New Mother's Guide

New Mother's Guide

to pregnancy and baby

Alison Mackonochie & Claire Cross

Illustrated by Claire Garland

MQP

Published by MQ Publications Limited

12 The Ivories
6–8 Northampton Street
London, N1 2HY
Tel: +44 (0)20 7359 2244
Fax: +44 (0)20 7359 1616
E-mail: mail@mqpublications.com

North American Office

49 West 24th Street
New York, NY 10010
E-mail: information@mqpublicationsus.com

Web site: www.mqpublications.com

ISBN: 1-84601-062-4

9 8 7 6 5 4 3 2 1

Every effort has been taken to ensure that all information in this book is
correct. This book is not intended to replace consultation with your doctor or
other health-care professional. The author and publisher disclaim any liability,
loss, injury, or damage incurred as a consequence, directly or indirectly, of the
use and application of the contents of this book.

Printed in China

Contents

Introduction

A baby is the most wonderful gift a couple can give to each other. Each little one who comes into our lives is a blessing; by the time you decide to start a family, you will want to know that you are doing everything to ensure that your baby has the best possible beginning in life. The *New Mother's Guide* was written to help, encourage, and comfort you as you experience one of the most special times in your life.

Pregnancy is an amazing and exciting experience, and one that will be enriched by knowing how your baby is developing—from the very beginning, when fertilization takes place, all the way through to the miracle of birth. Of course, pregnancy will change your body quite dramatically, and you will experience many new sensations—some of them good, others a bit more challenging. You can better cope with the very common ups and downs of these nine months by being aware of how and why your body is changing. In addition to being as physically ready as possible for pregnancy it's important that both you and your partner are prepared emotionally and practically for parenthood.

From the joyous moment when your newborn makes her entrance into the world to the celebration of her very first birthday, your baby undergoes unbelievable and miraculous changes. Each parent marvels at the weekly and even daily changes that transform the tiny, helpless bundle they brought into the world into a wonderfully chatty, confident, and independent toddler.

Watching your baby grow and develop over this first year is an experience that can be both exhausting and precious, and it features a few challenges and even more rewards. Understanding how your baby learns to walk, talk, and build up his repertoire of everyday skills will give you all the knowledge and confidence to encourage him with each brave new step he takes, making this first year a very special journey that you and your baby can enjoy together.

The *New Mother's Guide* will arm you with a wealth of information and ideas to make your pregnancy and the first months of your baby's life a very precious time that you will always cherish.

Preparing
for
pregnancy

Your health

If this is your first baby or you have had problems with a previous pregnancy—or if either you or your partner have any health concerns, now is the time to seek medical help and advice. Your doctor will be able to answer your queries and tell you how best to prepare yourself for pregnancy.

Get checked over

Ask your doctor for a checkup so that any physical problems you may have can be resolved before you become pregnant—it's a good idea for your partner to have a checkup, too. There are a number of tests that can be done to check for medical conditions that may affect your baby.

Blood tests and immunizations

You may be offered a blood test to check your immunity to rubella (German measles), an infectious viral disease that can cause malformations in a developing baby. If you are not immune you can be vaccinated—you'll be advised not to become pregnant until the vaccine virus has cleared from your blood, which takes about three months. A blood test may also be offered to confirm whether you carry the antibodies that will protect you and your baby from toxoplasmosis, an infection that is important to avoid when you are trying to conceive and during pregnancy.

If you've never had chicken pox (also called varicella) your doctor may suggest that you are immunized before you become pregnant. Ask your doctor to check the status of your tetanus vaccine, too—if you haven't had a booster in the past ten years, get one done now.

Medical conditions

Chronic illnesses, such as asthma, diabetes, and epilepsy, will need to be well controlled before you become pregnant, so ask your doctor for advice on how best to manage your illness. If you have a history of deep vein thrombosis (DVT), you will need to discuss any precautions you should take with your doctor before becoming pregnant.

If you have suffered from miscarriage, or had a stillbirth or a premature baby, or other obstetric difficulties talk to your doctor about any measures you can take that will help to carry your new child to full term. A history of genetic or chromosomal disorders in either your or your partner's family may necessitate a consultation with a medical specialist. Your doctor will be able to recommend a physician who can help you deal with this challenge.

Medications

If you are taking any prescribed medication, your doctor will be able to tell you whether the drug you are on is suitable for use during pregnancy. If it isn't, an alternative drug may be prescribed and you could be advised to refrain from conceiving until it is out of your system—which could take from one to six months. Once you start trying to conceive, be careful when taking over-the-counter medicines. Read all labels, and avoid any medicines that are not recommended for use during pregnancy. If in doubt, ask your doctor or a pharmacist.

Dental care

Research has shown that gum disease can increase the risk of premature birth, so see your dentist for a thorough examination and cleaning before you start trying to conceive. If you require dental work such as fillings or extractions, have them done now to avoid having to have treatment while you are pregnant.

Depression, anxiety, and stress

You are more likely to be fully fertile when you are emotionally healthy, so if you suffer from depression or anxiety you should seek treatment before you consider becoming pregnant. If your partner is depressed he is likely to suffer from a loss of libido and to find sexual arousal a problem. He may need help to overcome his depression before you start trying to conceive.

Try to lessen any pressures you are under and confront any problems you may have. Severe stress can upset the normal cycle of hormones produced by the pituitary gland, which in turn can inhibit ovulation. Encourage your partner to relax, too. Stress can affect testosterone levels, reduce the amount of sperm produced, cause premature ejaculation, or create difficulty in maintaining an erection—men under stress are also more likely to have poor sperm quality.

Weight

Check your weight—extremes on either side of normal can put a strain on your body, making it more difficult to conceive. You should be within 15 lbs (6.8 kg) of the ideal range for your height before you become pregnant. If you are underweight, there is a risk that your baby will be small and may have problems during labor and after the birth. Being overweight means that you are more likely to develop diabetes or high blood pressure during pregnancy. If your partner is significantly overweight, his testosterone production may be decreased, which can depress his libido.

If you need to lose weight, do it slowly and sensibly. Crash diets and other nutritionally unbalanced diets can lead to ovulation failure, a disturbed menstrual cycle, and ill health. They can also negatively affect your baby once you conceive.

Birth control

It is important to prevent pregnancy until you are ready for conception by using a method that doesn't affect your fertility. All hormonal contraception works by inhibiting the natural fertility cycle, and the time it takes for fertility to return to normal after stopping depends on the type you have been using. The body usually recovers quite quickly from use of the combined oral contraceptive pill, progestagen-only pill, implants, and the intrauterine device. However, if you have been having progestagen injections, it can take between six and 18 months for ovulation to return to normal.

Barrier methods such as the condom or diaphragm and spermicides are medically safe and instantly reversible, which makes them ideal for use during the pre-conception stage—although you may want to avoid the use of spermicides for a month or so before becoming pregnant.

Natural family planning—or fertility awareness—is another good form of contraception during this time and it has the added advantage of helping you to understand your fertility pattern. But it is important to remember that it can take between three and six monthly cycles to learn your fertility pattern, so this method should be combined with a barrier method until you are confident about using it.

Healthy living

Eating well, taking regular exercise, and avoiding health hazards during the months before you start trying for a baby will not only make you healthier and aid conception, but it will also stand you in good stead when you become pregnant.

Keeping fit and healthy

For optimum health you should cut back on junk food, refined sugars, and saturated fats and eat a nutritious, balanced diet that includes plenty of green and leafy vegetables, lean proteins, milk, and whole grains. Try to eat two servings of protein and three servings of calcium-rich foods every day.

The healthier your partner's diet, the healthier his sperm will be, so encourage him to eat nutritious foods, too. If either of you are vegan or if you are on a special diet, discuss your dietary requirements with your health-care professional.

Avoid infection

Because certain foods can harbor bacteria which can cause health problems that may affect a developing embryo— particularly during the vital early weeks of pregnancy—you should take care to limit your chance of developing food-borne infections such as listeriosis and salmonellosis during your preconception stage. You can reduce the risk of listeriosis by avoiding unpasteurized milk and soft and blue-veined cheeses, and by thoroughly cooking all meats and frozen or prepackaged dinners. To kill the listeriosis bacteria, heat foods to at least 160°F (70°C) for more than two minutes. (Remember, it's the food, not the oven, that needs to be at that temperature.)

Caffeine

Too much caffeine has been linked to infertility problems and increased risk of miscarriage, so try to have no more than 300 mg a day—3 cups of brewed coffee or six cups of tea.

Vitamins and minerals

Take a prenatal multivitamin supplement while you are trying to conceive—15 mg of zinc has even been shown to improve fertility in men. Never take more than one multivitamin supplement a day, as an excess of certain vitamins and minerals can be toxic. Vitamin B6 taken before conception and in early pregnancy has been shown to reduce the likelihood of morning sickness.

FOLIC ACID

This B vitamin is essential to cell growth and the development of an embryo. Take a daily supplement containing 0.4 mg of folic acid. All women of childbearing age should get this recommended amount, in case they unexpectedly become pregnant. If you have had a baby with a neural tube defect, or if you have epilepsy or diabetes, find out how much folic acid you should take before you become pregnant. You may require a higher dose. A low intake of folic acid has been linked to decreased fertility in men, so have your partner take folic acid daily.

Herbs

Some herbs, such as echinacea, ginkgo biloba, and Saint-John's-wort may prevent conception, so talk to your doctor about your herbal supplements. Some experts say that drinking clover flower tea and nettle tea helps to increase female fertility, while oat and sarsaparilla tea can increase male fertility.

Exercise

Follow an exercise program that tones and strengthens your muscles to help you carry your unborn baby more easily and prompt a smoother delivery. Regular exercise now will make it easier for you to continue exercising once you are pregnant and it improves the blood flow to your reproductive organs.

Long hours spent seated have been linked with lower sperm counts, so encourage your partner to move around when he is home. Sperm production can be impaired if the testicles overheat so your partner shouldn't wear tight clothing such as lycra shorts.

Personal considerations

Although you may be longing to become parents it's natural to have concerns about how you'll manage and what kind of parents you will turn out to be. Becoming parents will have a profound effect on the relationship between you and your partner—it can also alter your relationship with your parents and siblings. Talk about your feelings and discuss any concerns you may have as this will help to clarify your views on becoming parents.

FINANCIAL IMPLICATIONS

It's important to discuss with your partner the financial implications of having a baby before you become pregnant. Find out how much time your employers allow for maternity and paternity leave, as well as any financial benefits you might be entitled to. Work out your budget and talk to a financial advisor about the best way to plan for your baby's future. Make a will in which you name the people you want to be your child's guardians in case anything happens to you and your partner.

Conception

To conceive you need to make love around the time of ovulation—this is when an egg is released into the fallopian tube ready for fertilization by a sperm. If you have a regular 28-day menstrual cycle, ovulation will take place on around day 14. If your monthly cycle is irregular, working out your fertile period can be more difficult. An ovulation predictor kit can help you identify your fertile period, or you can learn fertility awareness. Conception takes place when a sperm penetrates the egg and fuses with its nucleus to form a single cell. This cell contains all the genetic information needed to create a new life.

The right time to make love

Once the egg is released it can survive for up to 24 hours, while sperm can live for two to four days inside a woman's body. The more frequently you have sex from day 11 to 16 of your cycle, the more likely you are to become pregnant. Deep vaginal penetration needs to take place to ensure that the sperm are deposited near or on the cervix, giving them the best chance of reaching the waiting egg.

Don't become disheartened if you don't become pregnant right away. Statistics show that about 70 percent of normal healthy people conceive within six months of trying, and that 95 percent conceive within two years.

Risks to avoid

Many of the health hazards you'll need to avoid during
pregnancy can also affect your chances of conception.

Chemicals

Some chemicals may affect your fertility or the health of your
unborn baby. Exposure to toxic chemicals can lead to loss of
libido, menstrual irregularities, and low sperm count. If you
work with chemicals and are not sure whether they could be
dangerous to you or your baby, check with the person at your
company who is responsible for health and safety or consult
your doctor. Wear rubber gloves when you are cleaning to
prevent the absorption through the skin of potentially
hazardous chemicals.

Paints

Although modern paint is lead-free some old paint contains
lead so you should wear a mask and gloves if stripping down old
paint. Even though the risk from paint is slight, exposure to lead
in large quantities can result in infertility in both men and women.

X-rays

Avoid any unnecessary exposure to X-rays or other forms of
radiation which could be harmful to your baby. If you are
actively trying to conceive, be sure to tell your health-care
provider that you could be pregnant.

Alcohol

Limit yourself to no more than one alcoholic drink per day during your preconception stage, and stop drinking completely once you start trying to conceive. Too much alcohol can disrupt your menstrual cycle and lead to other fertility problems. Heavy drinking is also thought to damage sperm and reduce their number. If your partner drinks heavily during the month before you conceive, there is a risk that this may affect the baby's birth weight.

Drugs

Don't use recreational drugs—these can be dangerous to your pregnancy and may hinder the chances of conception.

Smoking

You and your partner should give up smoking before you become pregnant. Smoking can reduce fertility and contribute to a low sperm count. Smoking has also been linked to low birth weight and premature birth and increases the risk of sudden infant death syndrome (SIDS) in newborns. If you are finding it difficult to give up, ask your doctor for help.

Temperature

Stay away from hot tubs, saunas, and electric blankets, as these increase your body temperature and might make conception more difficult as a result.

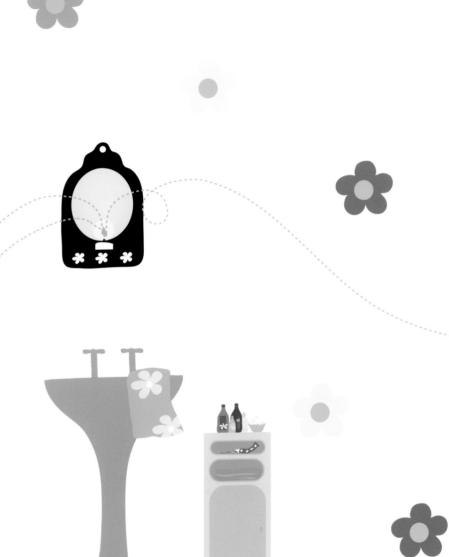

A happy pregnancy

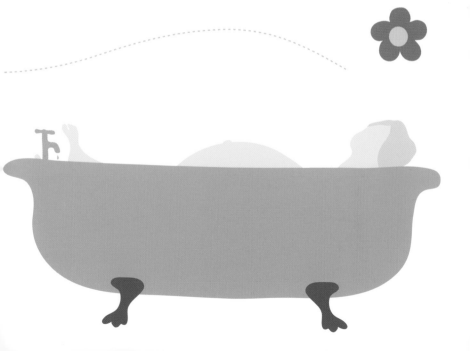

First trimester: weeks 1–12

Pregnancy is divided into three time periods called trimesters. Weeks 1 through 12 make up the first trimester; weeks 13 through 26 make up the second; and weeks 27 through 40 (or more, if your baby is late) make up the third trimester. Although you are unlikely to look significantly different during the first 12 weeks of pregnancy, momentous things are happening inside you as your body adapts to being pregnant. This is also a crucial time for your baby as it's during the first trimester that all his major organs are formed. One of the most important things to remember at this time is that although you might expect to feel elated and excited to be carrying your child, the hormones released during early pregnancy can make you feel tired and depressed.

How pregnancy is dated

Your pregnancy is estimated to be around 280 days—40 weeks long because it's dated from the first day of your last period rather than from when conception takes place. In reality, a full-term pregnancy is only 38 weeks long—266 days—because conception usually occurs about two weeks after the first day of your period. This means that by the time you've missed your first period you will be described as being in week four of your pregnancy, even though your baby will only be about two weeks old. It is at this stage that a pregnancy test will be able to confirm the pregnancy. Over-the-counter pregnancy kits are 99 percent reliable, and most can give an accurate result on the first day of a missed period.

How your body changes

You are likely to put on 2 to 4 lbs (0.9 to 1.8 kg) in the first trimester—but it is not uncommon to actually lose weight during this time if you suffer from morning sickness. By the end of your ninth week your uterus will have doubled in size, and you may notice that your clothes are starting to feel tight around the waist.

Circulation

Your blood volume starts to increase soon after conception so that your body can provide adequate blood supplies to the baby, the enlarging uterus and growing placenta. This means that your heart has to work harder to circulate the extra blood volume round your body. Toward the end of the second month your heart rate will have risen steeply. Your blood pressure is likely to fall during the first trimester, reaching its lowest level halfway through your pregnancy.

Metabolism

All your metabolic functions are increasing to provide for the demands of the growing baby, placenta, uterus, and lactating breasts. Over your pregnancy, your metabolic rate increases up to 25 percent. This increase may make you feel extra hungry, especially at night, when your blood sugar levels are likely to drop. The increase in circulation and metabolism affect many parts of your body, and can have a positive effect on your hair and nails.

Early pregnancy symptoms

Some women suffer from a wide range of physical symptoms during the early weeks of pregnancy, while others sail through with no problems at all. Pregnancy hormones are thought to cause of a lot of the unpleasant side effects of early pregnancy.

Tiredness (see also page 111)

This is very common in early pregnancy—in fact, you may feel absolutely exhausted most of the time. Although only temporary, get as much rest as possible until this feeling passes.

Tender breasts (see also page 108)

Your breasts will feel more sensitive than usual and may seem to be getting bigger. Tender breasts are one of the first signs of pregnancy and you may experience this even before you've missed your first period. As early as six weeks into your pregnancy, your hormones begin to stimulate your milk-producing glands in preparation for feeding your baby after the birth—you will also notice that your nipples have become more prominent.

Morning sickness (see also page 103)

Nausea affects around 80 percent of women in the early stages of pregnancy. Although called "morning sickness," nausea and/or sickness can occur at any time of the day. Some women never have morning sickness, but if you do, it will probably start when you are about six or seven weeks pregnant. In most cases, morning sickness begins to lessen at the end of the first trimester.

Frequent urination (see also page 114)

As the uterus expands it starts to press down on your bladder so that you have to make more trips to the bathroom than usual. This is likely to continue until the second trimester when the uterus rises up into the abdomen, taking pressure off the bladder.

Constipation (see also page 102)

Constipation is a common complaint in early pregnancy, and you may find that it remains a problem until after the birth of your child. It is caused by changes in your hormones that slow down your bowel movements. Constipation may cause gas and bloating early on, but this should ease as your pregnancy progresses.

Headaches (see also page 105)

Pregnancy headaches are quite common and are usually the result of hormone changes, fatigue, tension, hunger, or stress. It is best to avoid taking pain-killing medication during pregnancy, so find other ways to relieve the pain. If headaches are frequent or severe, you should contact your health-care provider.

Cravings

Studies show that up to 90 percent of expectant mothers experience a craving for at least one food. You are most likely to have cravings during your first trimester. A sudden aversion to a particular food or foods is also quite normal.

Excessive saliva (see also page 114)

An increase in the amount of saliva you produce is quite normal, and you may notice that it has a unpleasant metallic taste. Although the reason for this is unknown, it is more likely to occur if you suffer from morning sickness.

Vaginal discharge (see also page 115)

You'll probably notice an increase in vaginal discharge. As long as the discharge is white or clear, and odorless, there is nothing to be concerned about. If, however, the discharge becomes smelly or causes itching or soreness you should tell your health-care provider as this could be a sign of a vaginal infection that will need to be treated.

Your first prenatal appointment

Once your pregnancy has been confirmed you
will need to make an appointment to see your
doctor. This first prenatal appointment usually
takes place when you are 8 to12 weeks pregnant.
Your doctor will want to discuss your diet
and lifestyle, and you will be given a
physical examination, a blood pressure
check, and other routine tests to ensure that
you and your baby are healthy. If you suffer from a chronic
condition such as diabetes, your doctor will discuss the effect
of pregnancy on your condition and you are likely to be offered
more frequent prenatal checkups so that your health, and that
of your baby, can be monitored closely.

Blood tests

Your doctor will take a blood sample, usually from a vein in your
arm. This sample is used for a number of different routine tests,
which your doctor will explain. You may also be offered specific
blood tests to check for HIV and hepatitis B.

Urine checks

You will be asked for a urine sample at each prenatal
appointment. This will usually be checked while you are there,
using a specially impregnated dipstick. Your health-care provider
will test the urine sample for protein and glucose, both of which
could indicate a health problem.

Blood pressure checks

Your blood pressure will be checked for signs of pre-eclampsia at every prenatal checkup. This is a condition that affects about 8 to 10 percent of pregnant women. If left untreated it can cause serious problems for both mother and baby and in rare cases may develop into eclampsia, a life-threatening condition.

Weight and height

Your weight and height will be measured to calculate your body mass index (BMI), a medical classification for your body weight. If you are found to be in the normal range, your weight will probably not be checked again during the pregnancy, unless there are complications. If you are found to be overweight or underweight, you may need specialist care.

Checking your baby's growth

Your health care provider will palpate your abdomen and measure your fundal height—the distance from the top of your uterus to your pelvic bone. This gives an estimate of your baby's size.

Dating scan

Your health-care provider may offer you an early ultrasound scan known as a "dating" scan to confirm your due date and to check how many babies you are carrying.

Nuchal translucency scan

At between 11 and 14 weeks pregnant you may be offered a nuchal translucency screening to check for likelihood of Down's syndrome. The test uses ultrasound to measure the space in the tissue at the back of the baby's neck. Babies with abnormalities tend to accumulate more fluid at the back of their necks, causing the space to be larger. If the scan indicates that your baby may be at risk, you will be offered counseling and further diagnostic tests.

How your baby grows

By the time you miss your first period, your baby will be about two weeks old (you will be described as 4 weeks pregnant) and will measure between ¹⁄₇₀ and ¹⁄₂₅ in (0.36 and 1 mm) from head to foot. During the first few weeks of his life, your baby is known as an embryo. At this stage, he is made up of three layers of tissue, which develop separately. The outer layer becomes your baby's brain, nerves, and skin; the middle layer becomes his bones, cartilage, muscles, circulatory system, kidneys, and sex organs; and the inner layer becomes his breathing and digestive organs.

Your baby's development: weeks 4–10

Week 4 Your baby's heart can beat on its own—even though it's only the size of a poppy seed—and blood has started to circulate through his tiny blood vessels.

Week 5 His intestines are developing and his internal sex organs are almost completed.

Week 6 His eyes are open and his nose is beginning to form.

Week 7 His arms and legs are beginning to grow longer and he is capable of some movement.

Week 8 The foundations for all of your baby's body systems are now in place including the buds of all of his 20 milk teeth (often called baby teeth) which have formed in the gums. This is when your baby becomes known as a fetus rather than an embryo. This word comes from the Latin word that means "offspring."

Week 9 Your baby will begin to hiccup. Bouts of hiccups can last for several minutes, and by the time he reaches week 30 you will be able to feel them. Hiccups are thought to strengthen the diaphragm in preparation for breathing after the birth.

Week 10 Over the last three weeks he has doubled in size and now weighs between 8 and 14 g and measures 2½ in (61 mm).

The benefits of exercise

Taking regular exercise will strengthen your heart and lungs, improve your posture, boost your circulation, relieve muscle aches and cramps, help control your weight gain, reduce digestive discomfort, and strengthen your muscles. The calories burned during exercise will help to prevent too much weight gain. The fitter you are before you give birth, the more stamina you will have to cope with the stress of labor and the faster your recovery from the birth. Exercise during pregnancy will help you regain your shape more quickly once the baby is born.

Extra benefits

Physical activity also encourages the brain to release chemicals, such as serotonin, which help to balance the mood swings that are caused by an increase in your hormone levels during pregnancy. During exercise endorphins are released by your body, producing a calming effect that can last up to eight hours. After exercising you will experience a feeling of well being and your energy levels will be increased. It also has benefits for your baby. At the beginning of any exercise, your baby receives an emotional lift from the adrenaline that is pumped through your body. When your breathing is deep and your body is calm, your baby benefits from having extra oxygen.

Some studies suggest that exercise can help prevent gestational diabetes. For women who have already developed this type of diabetes, regular exercise—along with a change in diet— will help bring the disease under control. Another benefit is that it is thought that women who exercise regularly have faster labors and less need for induction.

Before you begin

Ask your health-care provider whether it is safe to continue any exercise program you followed before you became pregnant. Some modification is sometimes all that is needed for you to be able to continue with your program. Recent studies suggest that even vigorous exercise can be safe during pregnancy, provided that you are not having any health problems. However, it's not a good idea to take up a new sport while you are pregnant, although you may be able to continue with one you already do, providing your health-care provider approves of the activity.

Choose exercise clothes that allow you to move freely and wear a bra that gives your breasts plenty of support. Exercise wear should be made from fabrics that allow your skin to breathe, so avoid synthetic materials, which trap moisture to your skin, and choose instead garments made from cotton or other natural fibers. Wear shoes that are appropriate for the exercise you are doing. They should fit well so that they protect your feet and give your ankles plenty of support. Always exercise in a well-ventilated room.

Choosing the right exercise

Non-weight-bearing activities, such as swimming, cycling on a stationary exercise bike, and performing relaxation routines, can be done throughout pregnancy. Simply adjust your pace to suit your energy level and your stage of pregnancy. For example, during the first trimester you are likely to feel very tired, and you may also be suffering from a number of pregnancy discomforts. For these reasons, you shouldn't push yourself too hard to exercise a great deal (although you should exercise for at least a few minutes each day). If you were exercising before you became pregnant, you might want to maintain or reduce your exercise level during the first few months of pregnancy. If you are expecting twins, your doctor is likely to limit your exercise to non–weight-bearing activities that focus on toning and stretching your muscles.

You are much more likely to exercise if the activity you choose is fun. Choose a variety of activities each week to help keep you motivated. You may feel more motivated to exercise if you do it with others. Go to an exercise class, or walk, swim, dance, or perform some other aerobic activity with a partner or a friend. A small amount of exercise performed several times a day is better than one strenuous bout of exercise performed each week.

There are some forms of exercise that should be avoided during pregnancy, such as scuba diving, because of the risk of air bubbles forming in your baby's bloodstream, contact sports, and any other activity in which you could be hit in the stomach. High-risk activities such as horse riding or downhill skiing should also be avoided.

Aerobic exercise

All forms of aerobic exercise are good for your heart, lungs, muscles, and joints, and will help to build the stamina and energy you will need during labor. Unless your health-care provider forbids it, include some form of aerobic activity, such as a brisk walk or swimming in your daily exercise program. Walking and swimming are two of the safest forms of exercise, and you can continue doing them right up until the birth of your baby.

Exercises performed in water are ideal, as the water helps to support your weight so that you can work harder longer. Working out in water will prevent you from becoming overheated (provided, of course, that the water in the pool isn't too warm). Join an aqua-natal class, which focuses on exercises that have

been specially designed for pregnant women. Your health-care
provider or local community center may be able to help you
locate a class. If you go swimming, make sure you ease yourself
gently into the water. Refrain from diving or jumping into pools
and don't go swimming alone. Even if you are the only one in the
water, make sure that there's someone else around who can help
you if you have a problem.

Weight training

Weight training is good for building strength and toning muscles.
Be careful not to overdo it, though—use only light weights during
pregnancy so that you don't strain your muscles. During weight
training, remember to breathe out as you exert your muscles and
breathe in when you relax.

Kegel exercises

Exercise your pelvic-floor muscles on a regular basis by doing
Kegel exercises. To locate your pelvic-floor muscles, try stopping
the flow of urine midstream. The strength of these muscles is
determined by their ability to stop the flow. Once you have
identified the muscles you can exercise them at any time of the
day by simply tightening your pelvic floor and holding for a count
of five, and then letting go. Don't repeat the exercise during
urination in case your bladder doesn't empty fully which could
lead to a urinary infection. Kegel exercises should be done
throughout your pregnancy, as they strengthen the muscles in
the vaginal area and help to prepare them for
the birth of your baby. Strengthening the
perineal area will help to avoid tearing or the
need for an episiotomy—a cut to enlarge the
vaginal opening—during the delivery.

ABDOMINALS

Make simple abdominal exercises a part of your daily routine, as these will strengthen the muscles that protect your baby and your back. Exercises that you would normally do while lying on your back can usually be adapted so that you can sit, stand, or lie on your side after the fourth month.

Pilates

This form of exercise combines flexibility and strength training with body awareness and breathing. All the exercises are based around your central core—your abdominals and pelvic floor muscles. Some of the exercises are done lying on your front or back—positions which are not suitable from mid-pregnancy onward. Only do Pilates exercises that have been adapted for pregnancy. Get help with this from a qualified Pilates instructor.

Yoga

Yoga can help you relax, and it will improve your body awareness, but some positions should be avoided during pregnancy. Always check with a qualified instructor before including yoga in your exercise program. Some yoga positions are thought to help relieve indigestion and sickness. If you are suffering from digestive problems, ask your instructor about these. Yoga will teach you to focus, which will be of great benefit during labor.

Tai chi

Tai chi can help you relax and improve your body awareness. Check with a qualified instructor to make sure that the exercises you choose are suitable for pregnancy.

Stretches

Even if you don't feel like exercising, perform gentle stretches
to warm up your joints and muscles, stimulate your circulation,
and improve the oxygen supply to both you and your baby.
But be careful when doing stretches. Your joints will have been
loosened by pregnancy hormones, and they can be damaged
if you overstretch. Hold a stretch for no more than 20 or 30
seconds, and take care not to make bouncing movements when
performing any stretches.

BREATHING TECHNIQUES

Learn breathing and relaxation techniques during pregnancy so
that you can use them during the birth. Even if your pregnancy
is considered high-risk for medical reasons and you have been
told not to exercise, there is no reason why you shouldn't be
able to incorporate breathing and relaxation techniques into
your daily schedule.

Relaxation exercises

Get to know your body so that you know how your muscles feel
when you are stressed and when you are relaxed. You can learn
to reduce the stressful effects of day-to-day living by consciously
making yourself relax. It's easier to breathe when your shoulders
are relaxed so check for tension in this area throughout the day.
When practicing relaxation exercises, make sure that the room
you are in is warm, but not too warm, and that the surface you
are on is comfortable. You may find that soothing background
music helps you to relax. Before beginning relaxation exercises,
spend a few minutes just being quiet and gathering your thoughts.

Getting started

If you are not used to exercising, start slowly and build up gradually. Aim toward at least 30 minutes of moderate exercise each day. Always warm up thoroughly before you begin, and allow yourself a five-minute cool down period at the end of your exercise program. Remember to relax after you've finished exercising. You may find it more comfortable to exercise in the morning, when you are fresh and the air outside is still cool. Avoid exercising outside on hot days. If you are exercising at home, let the answering machine pick up incoming calls so that you are not interrupted during your program.

Have a drink and a light snack that's rich in complex carbohydrates, such as whole-wheat bread, 30 to 60 minutes before you begin a workout. Exercising on an empty stomach can make you feel faint and dizzy. Drink plenty of water before, during, and after any exercise program.

Measure your heart rate to gauge whether you are exercising hard enough. Find your pulse and count the number of beats you feel in 10 seconds. Multiply this figure by six to find out what your heart rate is for a one-minute period. Your instructor will be able to tell you what your target heart-rate zone should be during exercise.

Exercise safely

• Always stop if you experience any pain or discomfort, and seek medical assistance if you are at all concerned about the well-being of yourself or your baby.

• Stop exercising immediately and seek urgent medical attention if you start bleeding, pass fluid from your vagina, experience contractions, or have abdominal pains, or if you can't feel your baby moving.

• Remember that your center of gravity changes as your pregnancy progresses, and you are more likely to lose your balance. For this reason, you should avoid activities that put you in danger of falling.

• If you experience Braxton Hicks contractions—"practice contractions" that can become quite intense during the third trimester—while exercising, stop and rest until they are over.

• Take extra care when getting down onto the floor to exercise and returning to a standing position. Stand up slowly to avoid feeling faint.

• During the third trimester you will probably find that exercising gradually becomes more of an effort. Listen to your body and adapt your exercise regime accordingly.

• You should be able to carry on a normal conversation during exercise. If you can't, you are overdoing it.

• Make sure that you know how to do any exercise properly before performing it. Discuss anything you are not sure about with a qualified instructor. Poor form or an incorrect move can lead to injury.

• To protect your knees and ankles, always perform kneeling exercises on a folded blanket, an exercise mat, or soft carpet.

• If you ever feel faint, light-headed, or breathless while exercising, stop immediately.

• Avoid sit-ups or exercises where you have to raise your legs together while you are lying down, as this could damage your abdominal muscles.

• Don't get overheated because your body will take blood away from the uterus to help cool down the skin and this isn't good for your baby.

• Never exercise with just socks or tights covering your feet, as you may slip.

• Don't point your toes during exercise—this is likely to bring on a cramp.

• Never hold your breath during exercise, as this deprives your baby of oxygen. Try to keep your breathing at a controlled pace.

• Don't push yourself too hard if you are tired—it's important to listen to your body.

• Never exercise to the point of exhaustion, as the chemicals released by your body when it is overexerted are not good for your baby.

• Avoid doing exercises that jar your joints, such as high-impact aerobics and jogging.

• Exercises that require you to lie on your back shouldn't be done after the fourth month of your pregnancy. In this position, the weight of your uterus will press on blood vessels, which could restrict blood flow to your heart and to your baby.

• Avoid exercising on a surface that could jar your joints or cause you to fall.

Your dietary needs

During pregnancy, metabolic changes cause your body to make better use of the food you eat. Most pregnant women require only 2300 to 2500 calories a day—just 300 to 500 more than the number of calories required by women who aren't pregnant. This means that your daily extra calorie requirement can be met with simple snacks such as a bowl of cereal and a cup of low-fat milk; two slices of whole-wheat bread and butter or margarine, or an 8-oz glass of low-fat milk and a banana. Of course, not everyone has the same dietary needs, and the number of calories you should get depends on, among other things, your pre-pregnancy weight and fitness level. If you are concerned about your nutritional intake or you follow a restricted diet for medical reasons, always seek help and support from a dietician or your health-care provider as soon as your pregnancy is confirmed.

Getting the balance right

It is important to include foods that contain protein, fat, carbohydrates, minerals, and vitamins in your diet each day. Ideally, you should eat regular meals, starting with breakfast which really is the most important meal of the day. Try to limit your intake of fast food and prepared foods as much as possible, as these are usually low in nutrients and high in fat and salt.

If there are occasions when you have to miss a main meal, fill up by snacking on fresh or dried fruit, raw vegetables, muesli bars, or yogurt rather than cakes, biscuits, and sweets that have no nutritional value. Many working mothers-to-be find it helpful to keep healthy snacks in a desk drawer for a quick and easy "emergency meal."

Fruits and vegetables

Fruits and vegetables contain water and fiber as well as many important vitamins and minerals. You should eat at least five servings of these each day and try to include some raw vegetables and fruits. A serving is equal to one glass of orange juice, one large piece of fruit, or three tablespoons of a cooked vegetable.

Frozen and dried fruit and vegetables, which are picked at their prime and preserved within hours, often have more nutritional value than "fresh" produce that has been sitting on the supermarket shelves for a few days. Fresh vegetables lose their nutrients quickly, so try to eat them the day they are purchased. Where possible, eat these with their skins on them, as most of their nutrients are found just under the skin. Scrub the skins clean before cooking them.

Fruits and vegetables lose vitamins when they are sliced or cut, so eat them whole or in large pieces. When they are cooked vitamins leach into the cooking liquid, so use the water from boiled or steamed vegetables to make a gravy or a sauce. Organic produce is usually as chemical-free as it is possible to be in these times, so buy organic whenever you can.

Check the labels

If you buy ready-prepared foods, check that they don't contain unhealthy additives, that their protein content is adequate, and that food does not contain excessive amounts of sugar or sodium. Canned and frozen foods can be a healthy choice, provided they have no added sugar. (High fructose corn syrup is a sugar.) Check the sugar content of fruit drinks—some are pretty much pure sugar, with little nutritional value.

Vegetarians

If you are a vegetarian, you will need to ensure that you are getting enough protein, iron, calcium, B vitamins, and vitamin D. Vegetarians should eat a variety of protein-rich foods at each meal. You might, for example, combine whole-grain cereal with peas, beans, or lentils. Include soy foods, such as tofu and soybeans, in your diet, and eat plenty of eggs and cheese. If you don't eat dairy products, boost your calcium intake by eating plenty of dark green vegetables, such as broccoli and spinach, as well as soy products, dried figs, and seeds.

If you are a vegan, your health-care provider may suggest that you take a vitamin B12 supplement each day.

Essential nutrients

The best way to ensure that your diet contains all the nutrients you need is to eat a wide variety of foods from each of the food groups. Try to include something from each of the groups in your main meals every day.

Protein

Meat, poultry, fish, eggs, cheese, cereals, pulses, and nuts are the best sources of protein, which is needed to build your baby's cells, tissues, and organs. Protein foods have high levels of vitamins and minerals, such as B vitamins and iron. Some meat substitutes are good protein sources, but some are also high in fat and calories so always check labels, and choose products that are low in fat and contain 20 to 25 mg of protein per serving.

Essential fatty acids

Found in vegetables, seeds, nuts and their oils, lean meat, fish and fish oils, essential fatty acids are thought to be of particular benefit to your baby's development, especially during the last three months of pregnancy, when his brain increases four to five times in weight. Oily fish, such as sardines, salmon, and mackerel, contain omega-3 essential fatty acids, which are known to be important in the development of your unborn baby's brain and visual system. These nutrients also help to increase your baby's weight and reduce the risk of premature birth. There is some evidence to suggest that they can also reduce a woman's risk of high blood pressure during pregnancy. Eat at least two portions of fish a week—one of these should be oily, such as herring or sardines.

Carbohydrates

Breads, cereals, pasta, rice, and potatoes should form the largest part of your eating plan. Carbohydrates contain vitamins, minerals, proteins, and fiber, which are essential for both you and your developing baby. Unrefined cereals and grains, such as brown rice and whole-wheat breads and pastas, contain more nutrients and fiber than white breads and other refined products. Fiber is necessary for proper digestion, and it helps to prevent constipation.

Vitamin C

Found in citrus fruits, kiwi, cranberries, strawberries, papaya, red peppers, cauliflower, green vegetables, and potatoes, vitamin C is needed to help your baby to grow properly and to develop strong bones and teeth. Foods that are rich in vitamin C will also help you to fight off infections, and will enrich the placenta that nourishes your baby. Because your body can't store vitamin C, you need a fresh intake of it every day. Vitamin C is easily destroyed by light, heat, and exposure to air, so eat fruits and vegetables raw or lightly cooked to maintain as high a level of the vitamin as possible.

B vitamins

Foods that are rich in B vitamins, which are especially important in early pregnancy, include vegetables, whole grains, meat, fish, eggs, and milk. It's very important to take a supplement that contains folic acid—one of the B vitamins—not only before conceiving, but also during at least the first 12 weeks of pregnancy. Studies have shown that the risk of your baby having a neural tube defect, such as spina bifida can be greatly reduced by taking additional folic acid in supplement form. Folic acid is found naturally in foods, such as green leafy vegetables, oranges, and bananas, and a number of manufactured foods, such as some breads and cereals, have been fortified with folic acid, so increase your intake of these, too.

Vitamin A

Foods that are rich in vitamin A, such as red, yellow, and dark green leafy vegetables aid in the development of your baby's central nervous system. However, too much vitamin A can be toxic so avoid food containing high levels of the vitamin such as liver.

Vitamin E

Oily fish and most fresh fruits and vegetables are good sources of vitamin E, which is thought to boost your baby's immune response to allergens.

Iron

Good sources of iron include red meat, poultry, sardines, and dark green vegetables, such as spinach and collard greens; whole grains; nuts; eggs; and fortified bread and cereal. Iron is needed to produce new blood cells and will reduce your chance of developing iron-deficiency anemia. A diet that is rich in avocados, seeds, nuts, and vegetable oils may help prevent pre-eclampsia. Iron is more readily absorbed from dairy products and eggs than from plant sources such as spinach, so include plenty of these in your diet. Because vitamin C helps your body to absorb iron, it's a good idea to pair fruit or vegetables containing vitamin C, such as oranges, tomatoes, and red and green peppers, with iron-rich foods at meals.

Calcium

Calcium, one of the most important minerals to take during pregnancy, is needed to build your baby's teeth and bones and to develop his muscles, nerves, and heart. It also helps women reduce their risk of bone loss. Milk, cheese, and yogurt are all rich in calcium. Three 8-oz (225-ml) glasses of cow's milk will give you all of your daily calcium requirement. Recent research suggests that a calcium-rich diet may help to prevent pre-eclampsia and pregnancy-induced hypertension.

Help your body to absorb calcium more efficiently by increasing your intake of vitamin D. Eat dairy products, or include plenty of fortified bread and cereal in your diet. Calcium-enriched fruit juices are also good sources of this important mineral.

Magnesium

Many pregnant women suffer from low levels of magnesium. A diet that contains magnesium-rich foods, such as cereals, nuts, soy foods, milk, fish, and meat will help to maintain your magnesium level. Magnesium is thought to help prevent pre-eclampsia, and it may also reduce the number of cramps you experience.

Salt

Don't increase your salt intake, but don't restrict it, either—you will be losing more sodium through your urine as pregnancy progresses. Keep up your iodine intake by using iodized table salt.

Foods to avoid

Pregnant women should limit their intake of or completely avoid certain foods which have a high potential of carrying harmful bacteria that could cause problems in pregnancy and harm your growing baby. Common infections caught from contaminated food are listeriosis and salmonellosis, which have been linked to miscarriage, birth defects, and stillbirth. Less common is toxoplasmosis, which may cause miscarriage and birth defects.

Pâtés

Fresh meat, fish, and vegetable pâtés should all be avoided because of the risk of listeriosis.

Cheese and unpasteurized dairy products

Avoid mold-ripened and blue-veined cheeses, which carry a risk of listeriosis. Unpasteurized dairy products, sheep and goats' milk, and their products all carry the risk of toxoplasmosis. Always choose dairy products that are pasteurized.

Fish

Some fish, such as swordfish and king mackerel, may contain high levels of mercury, which could harm your baby's development. For the same reason, although the risk is considered minimal, you shouldn't eat more than two 6-oz (170-g) cans of tuna, or one medium-size fresh tuna steak, a week. Avoid raw fish and raw shellfish which may be contaminated with harmful bacteria. Limit your consumption of freshwater fish to no more than 6 oz (170 g) a week, and ensure that it has been very recently caught.

Eggs

Raw or undercooked eggs, and foods that contain raw eggs, such as mayonnaise, can be infected with salmonellosis which can cause serious stomach upsets. If you eat eggs make sure the yolk is solid.

Meat

Raw meat, such as Parma ham and salami, carry a risk of listeriosis. Undercooked meat and poultry carry harmful bacteria so make sure any meat you eat has been cooked thoroughly. Too much vitamin A can be toxic, so avoid liver and liver products which contain high amounts of this vitamin.

Unwashed fruit and vegetables

These—especially soil-grown vegetables—may be contaminated with toxoplasmosis, so you must always wash fruit and vegetables thoroughly before eating. Avoid alfalfa sprouts and other bean sprouts, which risk being contaminated with bacteria.

Peanuts

If you or anyone in your family has a history of food allergies, you may want to avoid eating nuts during your pregnancy and while you are breast-feeding.

Caffeine

Too much caffeine can increase the risk of miscarriage and result in a baby's low birth weight. Drink no more than three average-size cups of coffee or six cups of tea each day, and limit your intake of other caffeinated beverages, cocoa, and chocolate.

Alcohol

Most experts agree that it is best to avoid alcohol during the first trimester, when your baby's major organs are forming. If, after that, you decide to drink in moderation—no more than one unit a day—bear in mind that the alcohol will be passed to your baby through your bloodstream in the same concentration as it is in yours. If you drink heavily—five or more alcoholic drinks a day—during pregnancy, you are putting your baby at risk of fetal alcohol syndrome.

SUPPLEMENTS

Don't take supplements that have not been recommended or approved by your doctor. Even if you are advised to take supplements, it is important to remember that these should accompany—not replace—a nutritious, well-balanced diet. Vitamins and minerals taken in doses that exceed the recommended daily allowances (RDAs) can have a toxic affect on the body, which could be dangerous for you and your baby.

Fluids

Pregnancy boosts your body temperature, making it easy to become dehydrated, especially if the weather is hot. Drink at least eight 8-oz (225-ml) glasses of fluids every day. Water is your best choice, but milk, herbal teas, and fruit and vegetable juices are also good options. Try not to drink before you eat, or during your meal, as this will fill you up and make it harder for you to eat the amount of food you need at each meal for a healthy balanced diet.

Controlling your weight

Unless your doctor specifically advises you to do so, don't attempt to lose weight by restricting your caloric intake during pregnancy. Stay within the daily range of calories that your doctor advises. You need sufficient calories to enable your baby to grow.

If you are concerned that you are putting on too much weight, don't cut down on the amount of carbohydrates you are eating as they help you to feel full and give you energy. Instead, cut down on the sauces or other toppings that usually accompany them, such as butter, sour cream, and oily or creamy dressings.

Plan your meals and snacks in advance so that you don't become tempted by quick "empty-calorie foods"—foods that have little or no nutritional value—such as pastries, cakes, and sweets. You don't have to completely exclude junk foods such as chips, sodas, and candy from your diet—just limit them to the occasional treat.

No matter how much weight you put on, never be tempted to fast during pregnancy. Fasting during the last trimester is especially dangerous, as it can cause premature labor.

SAFETY AND HYGIENE

• Make dairy products, meat, poultry, and fish the last products you put in your shopping cart before heading to the checkout stand, so that they'll be out of the refrigerator for the least possible amount of time.

• Never eat food after its "sell by" date.

• Avoid buying food that is in damaged packaging, such as a dented can or a torn bag, as the preservation of the food may have been compromised.

• Store raw and cooked foods in separate sealed containers in the refrigerator. Place raw meats on the bottom shelf to avoid the risk of their juices contaminating other food.

• Thaw foods in the refrigerator or in the microwave (using the "defrost" setting). Never let foods thaw at room temperature.

• Don't refreeze food once it has been defrosted.

• If you reheat food, make sure that it is piping hot all the way through. Never reheat food more than once.

• Always wash your hands before preparing or eating food.

• Use a separate chopping board when you are preparing raw meat and poultry.

• After marinating raw meat, fish, or poultry, throw away the leftover marinade, as it may contain harmful bacteria.

Second trimester: weeks 13–26

Once you have reached this stage of pregnancy the risk of having a miscarriage is reduced by around 65 percent and many of the discomforts of early pregnancy will have passed.

Prenatal checks

If your pregnancy is considered low risk you'll be seen every month until 28 to 32 weeks, then every two weeks until week 36 when weekly checks are recommended until you give birth. If your pregnancy is high risk, you will be seen more frequently.

Pregnancy tests

There are a number of tests that you may be offered to check your baby's development and to see if he is healthy. These are optional and you should be clear about why they are being offered and if there are any risks attached to them before agreeing to have them.

Screening tests

These non-invasive tests (blood tests, for example, measure the levels of certain chemicals in your body) identify the risk of your baby having a defect such as Down's syndrome or spina bifida.

Diagnostic tests

These invasive tests carry a small risk of miscarriage. Tests, such as an amniocentesis, are offered if you are at high risk for a chromosomal abnormality—because your age puts you in the high risk group, or there is concern over the result of a screening test.

Ultrasound scans

You will be offered an ultrasound scan between weeks 20 and 24 to check your baby's development. This scan may be able to detect your baby's sex, but remember: it is not an exact science!

Common discomforts

Although morning sickness and fatigue are likely to have
lessened—or even disappeared completely—raised hormone levels
and the increasing strain your baby is putting on your body can
lead to other minor health problems.

Nasal problems (see also page 112)

High levels of the hormones estrogen and progesterone cause the
mucus membranes to soften and swell, which results in nasal
stuffiness and occasional nosebleeds. This condition often gets
worse as pregnancy progresses and then disappears after delivery.

Carpal tunnel syndrome (see also page 108)

Swelling tissues can press on the tendons and nerves in your
hands and cause numbness and tingling in your fingers in the
second and third trimesters. The condition ceases after the birth.

Clumsiness

Fluid retention and loosened joints can make your grasp less
firm so that you are more clumsy than usual.

Cramp (see also page 106)

Often worse at night, leg cramps commonly become more
frequent and painful as pregnancy progresses.

Edema (see also page 108)

Edema is an accumulation of fluid in the tissues. It commonly
occurs as swelling of the hands and feet. You are most likely to
experience this late in the day, in warm weather, or when you
have been standing for a long period of time.

Backache (see also page 107)

As your pregnancy progresses, the increase in weight and
changes in your center of gravity can put a strain on your back.

Itching (see also page 110)

Your abdomen may become itchy as it grows and the skin stretches over your expanding belly. If you experience itchiness all over, however, seek medical attention. This could be a sign of pregnancy-induced cholestasis, a rare but potentially dangerous liver disorder that requires urgent medical treatment.

Stretch marks

Stretch marks are thin, reddish lines that usually appear on the breasts, abdomen, and the tops of thighs. Because the skin is being stretched from the inside, creams and lotions will probably not prevent or reduce stretch marks, although they will help prevent your skin from feeling tight and itchy. Apply moisturizer to your skin straight after a bath or shower, while your skin is still damp. Minimize stretch marks by avoiding putting on excess weight, and drinking plenty of water so that your skin is hydrated. Stretch marks won't completely disappear, but they will, in time, fade to thin silvery lines. If you are going to get stretch marks, they will start to appear around week 26. You may also develop itchy pimples along your stretch marks. Known as pruritic urticarial papules and plaques of pregnancy (PUPPP), this usually disappears after delivery, and rarely reoccurs in subsequent pregnancies.

Varicose veins (see also page 115)

These often run in families and are more common in women than in men, so if there is a family history of them you are more likely to develop them during your pregnancy.

Braxton Hicks contractions

From about week 20 on you will start to feel Braxton Hicks contractions. Usually painless, these are your body's "practice" contractions, and they help to prepare the uterus for labor.

How your baby grows

Because your baby is floating in amniotic fluid, he is able to twist and turn and do somersaults. He uses his hands and feet to push himself off the muscular wall of your uterus, using it as a kind of trampoline. All this activity helps to tone and develop his muscles. As he gets bigger he has less room to move, so his movements slow down.

Your baby's development: weeks 11–24

Week 11 Your baby can sense sound through vibration receptors in his skin. Yawning and other jaw movements begin as early as week 11 or 12.

Week 12 Your baby can move his arms and legs, frown, smile, and suck his thumb.

Week 13 Extra-fine hair known as lanugo starts to develop all over his body. This helps to regulate his temperature. Lanugo usually starts to disappear at about week 28, although many babies still have a few fuzzy patches when they are born.

Week 14 Your baby's arms and legs are now complete and all his joints are working.

Week 15 His heart is pumping about 50 pints (24 liters) of blood a day.

Week 16 Your baby's unique fingerprints begin to develop.

Week 17 A thick, white, greasy substance called vernix is secreted by the glands in your baby's skin. This forms a waterproof barrier that prevents his skin from becoming waterlogged in the amniotic fluid.

Week 18 A baby girl will now have approximately six million primitive eggs in her ovaries. Many of these primitive eggs will degenerate before birth, so that by the time she is born the figure will be closer to one million.

Week 19 Your baby can hear and recognize your voice.
Week 20 Measuring about 7 in (19 cm) from his head to foot, your baby weighs about 12 oz (350 g).
Week 21 Your baby's fingernails are fully formed, and they continue to grow throughout the rest of your pregnancy.
Week 22 If your baby is a boy, primitive sperm will have formed in his testes.
Week 23 Your baby starts to develop his permanent teeth now, even though they won't appear until he reaches six or seven years of age.
Week 24 In preparation for feeding after the birth, your baby has learned to co-ordinate sucking and swallowing. The taste of your amniotic fluid is affected by your diet, so if it is artificially sweetened by something you've eaten, your baby will drink it twice as fast.

How your body changes

You can expect to gain about 12 lbs (5.4 kg) this trimester. By week 22 the top of your uterus can be felt close to your navel. If this is your first baby, you will probably start to feel her move somewhere between weeks 20 and 24. Emotionally, you should feel a lot more relaxed and happy.

Breasts

From about week 16 on, you will notice that your nipples and the areolas—the dark area around the nipple—have become darker. As your pregnancy progresses, the veins on your breasts will become more obvious as the blood supply to your breasts increases. Check your nipples at around 27 weeks to make sure that they are not flat or retracted, which will make breast-feeding difficult. If you are concerned, talk to your health-care provider about using nipple shields to help your nipples protrude.

Increased libido

You are likely to experience an increase in your libido. The additional hormones in your body boost blood flow to your pelvic area, making sexual arousal faster and more intense than usual. Unless your pregnancy is considered to be high risk, there is no reason why you shouldn't make love right up until you go into labor if you want to.

Skin changes

Some women develop a "bloom" during pregnancy—usually during the second trimester—so that their skin appears softer with a healthy glow. Others are not so lucky, and find that they break out in spots for the first time in years. The best way to treat pimples during pregnancy is with topical cleansers. Consult your health-care provider before using anything stronger—some acne treatments may be harmful to your baby. Never be tempted to squeeze pimples, as this will only make the problem worse. You can help control any outbreak of spots by cutting down on fats in your diet and by drinking plenty of water every day. If you do develop pimples and acne, rest assured that your skin will clear up once the baby is born, and your complexion should return to its pre-pregnancy state.

Both oily and dry skin benefit from exfoliation to remove dead surface cells, unblock pores, and stimulate circulation. Use cleansing grains or a mask every few days, or as recommended by the manufacturer, to give your skin an extra boost. If your lips are drier than normal, use a moisturizing lip balm to prevent them from cracking. Avoid the use of creams that contain a high proportion of vitamin A as there is evidence that an excess of vitamin A in the body could harm your baby.

MAKEUP

This can be a real morale booster when pregnancy makes you feel out of control of your body. Use makeup as a tool to help you feel attractive and more in control of how you look. Make sure that any cosmetics and skin-care products you use are suitable for your skin type.

Pigmentation

Dark areas of skin such as birthmarks and freckles may become darker if they are exposed to sunlight. You may even develop a butterfly-shaped patch of pigmentation across your face. This patch is known as chloasma, or the "mask of pregnancy," and appears on the forehead, cheeks, nose and chin. A good concealer will help to hide any skin discoloration and a UV sunscreen with a protection factor of at least 15 will prevent any further increase in pigmentation.

As your abdomen grows, you will probably notice a line of dark pigmentation down the center of it. This is due to the stretching of your rectus muscle. Don't be concerned; this line will disappear in the weeks after the birth of your baby.

Skin tags

You may develop a few skin tags—small floppy growths that appear in areas of high friction, such as under the arm. These usually shrink once pregnancy is over, but if you prefer, your doctor can remove them after the baby has been born.

MAKING A BIRTH PLAN

Make a birth plan by the end of your second trimester, as this will help you focus on and arrange for the type of birth you want. It's also a good way to identify any issues that you are unsure about, and will give you a chance to discuss your ideas with your health-care provider.

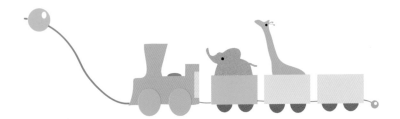

Hair

Your hair may appear thicker and glossier and you'll find a good, easy-to-maintain haircut will make life easier both during pregnancy and after the baby is born. Avoid hair dyes and other chemical treatments, such as permanents and body waves. Your hair's reaction to such treatments during pregnancy is likely to be unpredictable.

Sometimes pregnancy has the opposite effect on hair, making it appear dry and limp. Use a volumizing mousse to give dry, limp hair a lift and apply a hot-oil treatment or a deep conditioner once a week. Avoid using a hair dryer or other heated products, such as curling irons, which could further damage your hair if it is already thin and rather fragile.

If your hair become greasy, wash it frequently with a mild shampoo. Don't brush your hair too vigorously, as it will make oily hair even oilier, and it may result in more split ends for dry hair.

Hair removal

Even if you have used them without problem before, avoid the use of depilatories and bleach on unwanted body hair. Your skin, which is undergoing hormonal changes, may react differently to them during your pregnancy. Remove unwanted body hair by waxing or shaving. Electrolysis is generally not recommended, especially on the breasts and abdomen, although there is no evidence to suggest that it may harm your unborn baby.

Because of the hormones surging throughout your body, you may develop a bit of unwanted facial hair. This most commonly appears around the mouth, and on the chin and the cheeks. The best way to deal with these stray hairs is to pluck them.

Nails

Nails can also be affected by pregnancy and you may find that
they become longer and stronger than ever before. If you enjoy
long nails, make the most of them by keeping them well
manicured and polished. Alternatively, if your nails become
weaker and split and break easily, keep them short and wear
gloves to protect them when doing household chores and
gardening. Use a hand cream that contains a nail strengthener
to condition your nails and help keep your hands soft.

Eyes

Fluid retention can affect your eyes which can cause problems
if you wear contact lenses. Your optician can advise you on
whether you should switch to another type of lens, or if you
should wear glasses, until after the birth of your baby. If you
are bothered by dry eyes, ask your doctor for some lubricating
eyedrops. These will not only relieve your discomfort, but they
will also give your eyes a sparkle.

Teeth

Visit your dentist at the
beginning of your pregnancy,
and again six months later. Tell him
or her that you are pregnant so that you
aren't exposed to X-rays. See your periodontist as soon as you
know your are pregnant if you have had problems with your
gums in the past. Bleeding gums are common during pregnancy
so it's important to take special care to keep your teeth and
gums healthy. Clean below the gum line at least twice a day,
using a soft-bristled toothbrush, and floss regularly to remove
any trapped food from between the teeth. Gum disease shouldn't

be ignored as it has been linked to premature labor and if left untreated may lead to periodontal disease and tooth loss. Massage your gums with your toothbrush to help to discourage inflammation and infection.

Eating a nutritious diet and avoiding sweets and biscuits will help keep your teeth healthy. If you can't brush your teeth right after a meal, chew some sugar-free gum to prevent plaque buildup. Keep your breath sweet by brushing your tongue when you brush your teeth.

Feet

Your feet bear the brunt of the additional weight you are carrying so it really does pay to look after them by giving them a regular pedicure. Whenever you can, go barefoot at home as this will exercise the muscles in your feet and improve your circulation.

Procedures to avoid

• Don't get a tattoo or a body piercing while you are pregnant, as they could lead to infection.

• With all the changes that are going on in your body, now is not the time to consider having breast implants, and you are unlikely to find a doctor who would perform this type of cosmetic surgery while you are pregnant. If you already have breast implants, you are likely to experience discomfort, as the skin around your breasts is forced to stretch over both the natural tissue growth and the implant.

• Most dentists suggest that cosmetic teeth whitening should be avoided during pregnancy.

• Avoid cosmetic procedures, such as chemical peels and Botox and collagen injections, that contain chemicals that might affect your baby.

• It's best not to use a hot tub during pregnancy, as the hot water will raise your body temperature which may be hazardous to your baby.

• Using a sauna or steam room are not advisable during the first trimester and you should check with your health-care provider before using these facilities later in pregnancy.

Fashion sense

What you wear during pregnancy will probably depend on how you feel about your changing shape. You may be happy in figure-hugging outfits that emphasize your belly, or you may prefer loose garments that have ample room for growth. There are no taboos when it comes to pregnancy fashion, so choose a style that feels right for you. Maternity clothes have been specially designed to grow with you, so they should look good throughout your pregnancy.

Your basic wardrobe

You may not need to purchase any maternity clothes until you reach your second trimester, and even then you may be able to get away with a few items that are a size or two bigger. It's best to put off buying your maternity wardrobe until you really need it as you are likely to be wearing these clothes for the rest of your pregnancy. To get a variety of "looks" without breaking the bank, buy a few basic garments that are interchangeable and add some unusual accessories that will add interest to your pregnancy wardrobe and give you a boost. You can often find good bargains on maternity clothes at second-hand stores.

If you opt for figure-hugging pregnancy clothes, choose comfortable garments made of stretchy fabric. Sweat suits make comfortable lounging-about-at-home wear. Don't buy clothes that have tight elastic waistbands, as these will be uncomfortable and may also restrict your blood flow, and avoid man-made fabrics that trap the sweat against the skin.

Dress in layers in the winter, so that you can take clothes off when you heat up and add another garment when you're feeling cool.

Underwear

Wear a good, well-fitting bra throughout your pregnancy to give your breasts the support they need. Find a store that offers a bra-fitting service, so that you can be sure the bra you buy is the correct size. Always buy a new, correctly sized bra as soon as the one you are wearing begins to feel tight and uncomfortable.

Choose a bra that has a broad band under the cups that will give your breasts support as they become heavier. Look for one that has four hook-and-eye fastenings so that you can loosen it as your ribcage expands. Don't wear underwire bras, as they may damage delicate breast tissue. At about week 36 you may want to buy a nursing bra if you intend to breast-feed. These come in two basic types—those with a front opening that exposes only the nipple area and those that unfasten to expose the whole breast. If your breasts are particularly large and heavy, you might be more comfortable sleeping in a lightweight maternity bra or a specially designed sleep bra.

You'll find bikini briefs the most comfortable choice when it comes to underwear, because they fit under your belly. Maternity tights fit comfortably over your bump and will give your legs some much-needed support during the last months of your pregnancy. Don't wear stockings with garters, thigh highs, or tight socks, as these may restrict the blood flow to your legs and cause varicose veins.

Shoes

Your feet will get bigger toward the end of your pregnancy. Be prepared to buy shoes with low heels, that are wider, or even a half-size larger. Always buy new shoes in the afternoon, when your feet are likely to be at their biggest. This way, you can make sure that they won't become uncomfortable when your feet swell. When trying on shoes, walk around in them before you purchase them and take your time to ensure that the shoes are comfortable and that they fit properly. Shoes should be made from breathable material as your feet are likely to sweat more than usual. Alternate the shoes you wear each day to give each pair a chance to dry out before you put them on again. Avoid laces and buckles on shoes which will become a nuisance in later pregnancy when you'll find it difficult to reach your feet.

In addition to everyday shoes you'll need a pair of cross trainers that feature good foot and ankle support for exercise.

QUICK PICK-ME-UPS

• Reduce puffiness around your eyes, caused by fluid retention, by placing cotton pads soaked in witch hazel on your eyelids.

• To refresh tired eyes, place cold cucumber slices or pad soaked in ice-cold water on your eyelids and lie down for ten minutes.

• If your feet and ankles swell toward the end of the day, sit with your feet up whenever you can. Although you won't be able to get rid of the swelling completely, this will help to minimize it.

• Revive tired feet by soaking them in a bowl of warm water, then massage them with peppermint foot cream.

• Create a bedtime routine that will help you unwind.

• Drink a glass of warm milk before bedtime as this really does help you to fall asleep. Tryptophan, a naturally occurring amino acid that promotes sleep, is released when the milk is heated

• Cleanse your face and neck thoroughly each night, and take the opportunity to relieve tension by massaging your temples.

• Make time to relax each day, even if it's only for half an hour.

Preparing for your baby

One of the most enjoyable parts of pregnancy is planning the nursery and shopping for your new baby. These are areas where your partner can really become involved so that you can enjoy doing them together. One of the most fun items to buy are cute baby clothes. It is best to buy a minimum of newborn-sized clothes, as babies grow out of them very quickly. In fact, if your baby is large—around 10 lbs (4.5 kg) at birth—he will probably already be too big for newborn clothes. Remember, too, that you are likely to be given clothes as presents when your baby arrives.

Basic layette

It's so tempting to splurge on gorgeous baby clothes, but remember that your baby will grow quickly—if you buy too many in one size, he may not have time to wear them all! Furthermore, you will more than likely be inundated with baby clothes from family and friends so assess your baby's wardrobe once all gifts have been received, then stock up on any missing items.

Your baby's wardrobe

Your baby needs a fairly simple wardrobe. In the first few months, tops and sleepsuits suffice for both day and night, with a couple of cardigans or a jacket added for extra warmth in the winter months. Don't break the bank buying baby clothes. Check out second-hand baby shops and happily accept hand-me-downs from family and friends. Babies grow out of clothes so rapidly that many second-hand clothes are as good as new.

DRESSING FOR THE WEATHER

Check to see whether your baby is too hot or too cold by touching his skin. If his hands and feet feel cool, he probably needs extra layers of clothing whereas moist skin on his head, neck, and chest could mean that he is overdressed. On hot summer days, a diaper and a top may be all that your baby needs indoors, but cover him when he is outside to protect him from the sun's rays. Choose clothes that are 100 percent cotton—they're gentle on your baby's soft skin, and they help to prevent him from overheating. In the winter months you can keep your baby as warm as toast by wrapping him up in a snug snowsuit.

Keep it simple

Make dressing your baby hassle-free. Tops that have envelope-style necks can be stretched before slipping them over his head so that he doesn't get distressed by material being dragged over his face. All-in-one stretchsuits with snaps that fasten between the legs are easy to use; they won't ride up, leaving your baby with a chilly tummy and are ideal when it comes to diaper-changing as you don't have to remove any clothing. Avoid clothes with complicated ties and buttons.

Natural fabrics

Your baby's clothes should be made of natural materials to minimize sweating and skin irritation. Fabrics are sometimes treated with chemicals during the manufacturing process, and these may irritate your newborn's delicate skin. Wash, rinse, and tumble dry all of your baby's new clothes before you put them away in preparation for her arrival.

The nursery

Although your baby may share your room for the first few months
of her life, it's a good idea to prepare the room she's eventually
going to sleep in well before she arrives. This will give you plenty
of time to plan the layout, decide on furnishings and color
schemes, and to buy the essential items you'll need for your baby.

Decorating

Paint is a far more practical choice than wallpaper for your baby's
room, as the walls will probably need to be washed frequently.
Choose a paint that has a satin finish, which holds up well after
being washed. The nursery must be completely free of paint
fumes and other potential hazards before your baby sleeps there,
so any painting should be finished well before your due date, and
leave the windows open so that fresh air can circulate.

If you plan to decorate the nursery yourself, remember that
your balance isn't as good as it used to be, so take care on
stepladders, and don't try to reach up too high. It is all too easy
to become unbalanced and fall. It's not good for you to breathe
in paint fumes either, so try to get someone else to paint the
nursery. If you must do it yourself, wear a protective mask and
use a water-based paint rather than one that is solvent based.
Old paint often contains lead, which is toxic. For this reason,
under no circumstances should you sand or scrape any paint if
you are at all unsure about its age or chemical content.

Choose decorations for the nursery that can be adapted as
your child grows. Brighten up plain walls with colorful friezes or
stencils that are easily changeable to more suitable designs as
your child gets older.

Lighting

The nursery should have a bright overhead light for use during your baby's waking periods. Softer, less intrusive lighting is better for nighttime changing and feeding. You can get both from one source by fitting the ceiling light with a dimmer switch. You may also want to consider purchasing a night-light that is made for use in the nursery. This will give out a comforting glow that will help to settle your baby at night.

Choose thick curtains for the nursery or put up a blackout blind that will help to keep out early-morning light. These can also be useful when you want your baby to go down for a nap during the day.

Nursery furnishings

The furniture that you buy for your baby's room should be sturdy enough not to be pulled over once your baby is standing and moving around on her own. A changing table that is designed to hold diapers and toiletries is a useful piece of nursery equipment, and will help prevent your back from becoming strained when you change your baby. If you haven't room for a changing table, invest in a padded changing mat. This can be used on the floor or on the bed and makes a great place for your baby to lie and kick without her diaper on. Never leave your baby alone when you're changing her, especially on the bed or a changing table as she could easy roll off and hurt herself. A thermostatically controlled heater will allow you to keep the nursery at the right temperature—65°F (18°C). You may also want to add a wall thermometer which will enable you to keep a check on the room temperature to ensure that it remains constant.

A place to sleep

Your newborn will need a comfortable and safe place to sleep, such as a Moses basket, a cradle, or a crib. Moses baskets and cradles can be used for babies up to about four months of age, and because each takes up less space than a crib, one of these may be more suitable if space is at a premium. A standard-sized crib will last your baby from birth to the time when she is old enough to go into a bed. Look for a crib that allows you to adjust the mattress height so that the mattress can be raised high enough to allow you to easily lay the baby in the crib (but not so high that she could fall out of it). This is safer for your baby, and it will help protect your back, too. Make sure that the crib's side rails are no more than 3 in (8 cm) apart so that there is no risk of your baby's head becoming stuck between the rails. Avoid crib bumpers; although these prevent your baby from banging her head on the crib bars, they can cause her to overheat, and when she gets older she could climb on them and fall out of her crib.

Some cribs convert into a bed that can be used when your child becomes a toddler. Before you decide on one of these, consider whether you are planning to have more children. If so, you are going to need a crib as well as a bed at some stage, so this may not be the ideal choice.

Mattress

Always buy a new mattress for a crib. Don't use a second-hand mattress, even if the only other person to use it was a previous child of yours. The mattress your baby sleeps on should fit snugly so that there is no risk of your child becoming trapped between it and the sides of the crib. Choose a vinyl-covered mattress, which is water resistant.

Bedding

Buy three sets of bedding, so that you can have one on the crib or Moses basket, one dirty or in the wash, and one clean and ready to be used. Choose bedding made of natural materials to minimize sweating and skin irritation. Check the care labels on bedding before you buy them. Your baby is likely to need changing several times a day, and you won't have time to hand-wash or iron bedding. To remove potentially harmful chemicals from newly purchased bedding and towels, wash, rinse, and tumble dry them before you put them away in preparation for his arrival.

Don't buy quilts, comforters, or pillows for the crib, as these could cause your baby to overheat or suffocate. Comforters and pillows have been linked with crib death, or sudden infant death syndrome (SIDS). If your older baby wriggles out of her blankets, keep her snug in a cotton sleeping bag. Specially designed for babies, these may give you and your baby some welcome, uninterrupted sleep. Keep a supply of clean sheets and blankets close to your baby's crib so that you can change wet sheets in the night in a matter of moments. Some cribs come complete with covers and frills. Although these look attractive, they are potentially dangerous, so avoid or remove ribbons or other frills that could strangle your baby.

Baby food

You will spend a lot of time in the early months feeding your baby, so it's a good idea to think about how you are going to feed your baby now. Discuss the benefits of breast-feeding over bottle-feeding with your health-care provider. She or he will help you make this important decision.

Breast-feeding

Breast milk is the perfect food for your baby because it contains everything your baby needs, in the right proportions, for the first six months of his life. Breast milk is easy for your baby to digest, is readily available, and is always at the right temperature—and it's free. As your baby grows, your breast milk will adapt to his different requirements. To breast-feed you will need the following equipment: breast pads; bottles and nipples (for expressed milk); sterilizing equipment; a bottle brush; and a breast pump. Breast milk can be expressed by hand, but you may find it easier and quicker to do with a breast pump.

Benefits for your baby

Colostrum, the first "milk" your breasts produce, plays an important part in keeping your baby healthy because it contains antibodies that help to protect your baby from infections and harmful bacteria Research indicates that babies who are breast-fed are less likely to develop childhood diabetes and allergic conditions such as eczema. Breast milk is known to contain vital long-chain polyunsaturated fatty acids which play an important part in your baby's brain development. It is also less likely to make your baby overweight, and it may help to prevent obesity later in life.

Benefits for you

Breast-feeding has benefits for you, too. It helps burn off fat that you have accumulated during pregnancy, and it encourages the uterus to shrink back to its pre-pregnancy size more quickly. Breast-feeding for at least six months significantly reduces the risk of pre-menopausal breast cancer, and can protect you from osteoporosis and ovarian cancer.

Bottle-feeding

If you can't or don't want to breast-feed, you will need to give your baby formula. Although they don't offer the same degree of protection as breast milk, infant formulas have been developed to provide your baby with the right balance of vitamins and minerals that he needs to thrive for the first six months. There are a number of brands to choose from, most of which are made from modified cow's milk. Don't buy formula too far in advance of using it, and never use formula that is past its "sell by" date.

To bottle-feed you will need the following equipment: bottles and nipples; sterilizing equipment; a bottle brush; a bottle warmer (optional); and formula. A sterilizer is a must for bottles, nipples, and pacifiers.

MIXED FEEDING

If you decide to try to combine breast-feeding and bottle-feeding with formula, you will need to wait until breast-feeding is established before giving formula to your baby. When you introduce your baby to the bottle, use natural-shaped or orthodontic-shaped nipples, as these provide a sensation that is most like sucking from the breast.

Diapers

When considering your choice of diaper, you need to take into account the cost, how much time you have available for washing and drying, your washing facilities, and your concern about the environment. Disposable diaper liners can be used with either towelling or reusable diapers to help prevent diaper rash, and to make diaper changing easier as any soiling can be removed and flushed down the lavatory.

Disposable diapers

Disposable diapers are convenient, but their cost is very high, considering that your child is likely to use up to 6000 diapers before he's potty trained. It is generally considered that disposable diapers are less environmentally friendly, because some of their man-made materials can take up to 500 years to decompose. Invest in a diaper container that seals used disposable diapers in film wrappers so that there is no smell. These devices can store several days' worth of diapers before being emptied into the wastebasket.

Cloth diapers

Cloth diapers are high-maintenance—they require sterilizing, washing, drying, and airing after each use. But around a dozen cloth diapers will see you all the way through the diaper stage of your child's life. Shaped, reusable cloth diapers are softer than ordinary towelling ones and they are easier to put on. They often come with Velcro fastenings, so you don't have to use pins or clips to secure them. Reusable cloth diapers are considered more environmentally friendly than the disposable kind but bear in mind that the detergents needed to clean them also have an environmental impact.

Baby gear

When it comes to buying baby equipment, the choice is enormous and it's easy to be seduced by attractive designs and colorful fabrics into buying items that you don't really need. It's a good idea to ask other parents about the equipment that they really found useful and where possible to borrow equipment that will be used for a very short time, such as a cradle or a "bouncy chair." Be on the lookout for second-hand baby equipment that's in good condition, as this can save you quite a lot on money. Most newborns grow out of things very quickly, so it's usually quite easy to pick up some bargains.

Always check baby equipment to make sure that it conforms to accepted or required safety standards. This should be clearly marked on all items of equipment whether it's new or second-hand. Don't be tempted to buy equipment that is substandard, even though it may appear to be a bargain. It may not be safe, and you could be putting your baby at risk.

When buying new, you can save yourself time and energy by buying from mail-order firms and Internet companies that specialize in baby clothes and equipment. Not only are their prices often quite competitive, but they will deliver the merchandise right to your door, as well. If you are superstitious about buying baby equipment, such as a carriage, before the birth, ask if the store will accept a deposit and deliver once your baby arrives.

Baby monitors

A baby monitor allows you to keep tabs on your baby, even when he's asleep. Baby monitors come with baby and parent units, and most can be operated by battery or by regular electricity. Some have night-lights on the parents' unit, others come with a sound-activated night display screen. More sophisticated models include a temperature indicator on both units, an out-of-range alarm, and a low-battery warning light. Always check the range and reception of your baby monitor as soon as it is purchased.

If you want more reassurance than that offered by a regular baby monitor, consider a monitor with a sensor pad, which is placed under your baby's mattress to monitor your baby's movements and breathing.

Car seats

One of the first pieces of equipment you will require is a car seat so that you can safely transport your baby home from the hospital. An infant car seat can be used from birth until your baby weighs about 29 lbs (13 kg)—most babies are about six months old at that point. The seat is held in place by the seat belt and it faces the rear of the car, which gives your baby maximum protection.

When purchasing a car seat, consider how easily the harness adjusts; whether the covers are easy to remove and are washable; whether the seat reclines; and how well it supports your baby's head. Choose one that combines comfort and safety with a buckle that is easy for you—but not for your baby—to undo. Most have large side wings, which give maximum protection from a side collision. Always fit the seat in accordance with the manufacturer's instructions. If you are in any doubt about the fitting, take the seat and the car to a garage that offers a baby-seat fitting service. Not all car seats fit all cars, so check that the one you are thinking of buying is suitable for your vehicle. Never buy a second-hand car seat, as it may have been damaged and could put your baby at risk.

Your baby can be easily moved from the car to indoors in a car seat that doubles up as an indoor seat, some of which have a rocking mode that your baby will love. When you buy a car seat, ask the assistant to show you how to fit it in your car before you attempt to do so on your own.

Carriages and strollers

Before buying a pram or stroller think about your lifestyle—where you live and your usual way of getting about. If you are going to be walking around town every day, and if you are planning on having more than one child, consider buying a traditional carriage. These offer a comfortable ride, and they are long lasting. If you drive a lot or if you use public transportation, select a stroller that can be easily maneuvered, lifted, and folded. An all-terrain three-wheeler may suit you if you do a lot of country walking, or if you are an avid jogger. When selecting a carriage or a stroller, check the equipment's recommended age range to make sure that it is suitable for a newborn.

Strollers or buggies

Modern strollers are truly versatile. Many feature fully reclining seats that can be used from birth, then adjusted to suit your baby as she grows and is able to sit up. However, umbrella folding buggies and strollers are not suitable until your baby is six months old and can sit up comfortably on her own. Keep your newborn safe and snug by choosing a stroller with safety straps that fit over her shoulders and around her waist. Before you buy a stroller, make sure that the one you have chosen fits easily into the trunk of your car. Treat your small baby to some brightly colored stroller toys and your older baby to a board book attached to her stroller to keep her amused as she cruises along.

Traditional baby carriages

These help protect your baby from car fumes and cold drafts, but they can be bulky and cumbersome on public transportation and difficult to fit into cars. Some carriages have a removable crib, which allows you to bring your sleeping baby indoors without having to disturb her.

Slings and carriers

Your newborn will enjoy being held close to you so that he can hear the familiar and comforting sound of your heartbeat. Because it's impractical to carry your baby around in your arms when you are busy around the house or out shopping, a baby sling is a wonderful investment. Choose one that is made from machine-washable padded cotton and which offers your baby good head and back support. Always try a sling on before you buy it to make sure that you can get it on and off easily. Framed back carriers are more substantial than baby slings, and they are better for older, heavier babies. When your baby is awake, put her face out in the baby sling so she can watch the world go by.

SECOND-HAND

Although buying second-hand can save you a lot of money,
it's important to check that the pram or stroller hasn't been
damaged in anyway, as this could put your baby at risk. Be sure
to obtain the operating instructions and to get the brakes tested
to make sure they work properly. You will also need to purchase
a new mattress for a second-hand carriage.

Toiletries

Your newborn's skin will be very soft and delicate, so it is best not
to use soap on it until she's at least three months old. Plain warm
water and cotton balls are that are needed to "bathe" your new
baby. As your baby is likely to be born with some dry patches you
may need baby oil and baby moisturizer. You will also need some
form of barrier cream, such as petroleum jelly, to help prevent
diaper rash. Always choose hypoallergenic, dermatologist-tested
baby toiletries, which will be kind to your baby's skin.

Bathtime

A baby bath is not an essential piece of
equipment, but it does make bath time easier.
Alternatively, you may want to consider buying a
specially designed bath support that fits into the bathtub.
This will keep your baby's head well above the water, leaving
your hands free to wash him. A bath thermometer can be useful
as it changes color to indicate safe and unsafe heat levels. For
your baby's bath time you will need: cotton balls; baby wipes;
large soft towels; a flannel cloth or a sponge; a soft hairbrush;
and blunt-ended scissors.

Other issues

Use this time, while you are waiting for your baby to arrive, to address the practical and emotional changes that are taking place, and to consider the effect that having a baby will have on you and your partner's lives in the future.

Your relationships

Pregnancy is not without its emotional ups and downs and it's important to keep the lines of communication open between you and your partner, and to talk to each other about your feelings. Your partner may feel rather left out as everyone lavishes attention on you during this time and he may need reassurance that he's still as important to you as he was before you became pregnant. Try to make a special effort to include him, as much as possible, in your prenatal experiences so that he can feel part of your pregnancy.

Older children

If you already have a child you may find that he or she feels insecure about the fact that a new brother or sister is on the way. Reassure your child that your feelings for him aren't going to change, and explain how important he will be to the new baby. You can help prepare your older child for the new arrival by letting him feel the baby move inside you, and by encouraging him to talk to his new sibling.

Families and friends

It's a good idea to involve the future grandparents as much as possible now to help them feel that your unborn baby is already part of their lives. In fact, it's quite natural to find that you feel especially close to your parents and parents-in-law during pregnancy. Families often give much needed support during pregnancy, especially if you don't have a partner around to help, so accept as much help as you need, and don't be afraid to ask for it if necessary. If you don't have family to fall back on, check out local or Internet-based groups and organizations that may be able to put you in touch with other similarly placed parents, as well as offer practical and emotional support.

Sex

Pregnancy affects couples in different ways. Some men find the sight of a swelling abdomen very sexy, while others consider it a real turnoff. However your partner feels, try to be understanding.

You may find that you lose interest in sex during the first trimester, especially if you are feeling exhausted and suffering from morning sickness. If this is how you feel, explain to your partner so that he understands and tell him that you would prefer to have a lot of cuddling instead.

Many women find that they feel especially sexy during the second trimester and some experience multiple orgasms for the first time during this stage of pregnancy. Rest assured that intercourse will not hurt your baby, and make the most of your increased libido. Toward the end of your pregnancy you may find that your expanding belly makes some positions awkward, uncomfortable, or difficult to achieve. Try experimenting with positions that keep your partner's weight off your stomach. Having sex is a good way to tone muscles in preparation for labor as intercourse exercises the pelvic floor, and during orgasms, the muscles of the uterus are exercised.

Your emotions

Pregnancy is a time of great change, both physically and emotionally, and it's not uncommon to sometimes feel as though you've become a completely different person. Don't be surprised if you feel "up" one minute and "down" the next. Mood swings are a natural part of pregnancy. However, some women experience prenatal depression so if you are depressed for more than a couple of weeks, seek medical advice.

It's easy to feel that all people see when they look at you is a pregnant woman, and not the real person underneath the belly. Take time out to look after yourself, pursue your own interests, and make the most of the benefits that pregnancy often brings, such as glossy hair, glowing skin, and healthy nails. It's important for you to experience pregnancy in a way that makes you happy. Research suggests that your baby experiences your feelings of happiness, relaxation, and freedom from stress through chemicals released into the blood stream. So, if you feel maternal early on, indulge yourself and enjoy buying baby clothes, outfitting the nursery, or knitting tiny baby garments. If you prefer instead to focus on your "normal" life and to carry on as usual during the early months, that's fine, too.

It is quite normal, too, to have doubts about your pregnancy, about whether you will be a good parent, or even about whether your baby will be healthy. It may help to share these feelings with your partner or with other mothers. Once these doubts are out in the open, they often become less worrying.

One of the advantages of prenatal care is the reassurance it can give you. Your health-care provider will offer positive information about your baby's development and your own health, which will help to relieve any worries you may have. Vivid dreams about your unborn baby are likely to have been caused by anxieties that are normally suppressed when you are awake. It is quite natural and common to have such dreams, but some women become alarmed and wonder whether their bodies are trying to tell them that something is wrong. Don't be embarrassed to discuss your fears with your health-care provider, who should be able to put your mind at rest.

BONDING

You and your partner can begin bonding with your baby long before her birth by stroking your belly and talking and singing to your unborn child. If you are supportive of each other during pregnancy, you and your partner should find that bonding with your baby comes naturally after the birth.

Parenting classes

Remember you're not alone here and there are plenty of organizations that can help you to better understand the journey that you are just about to embark upon. Many health-care providers offer childbirth and parenting classes, but they often must be booked well in advance.

These classes give you the chance to talk to other parents-to-be, as well as the opportunity to talk with a health professional about any concerns you may have. The best way to minimize any fears that you or your partner may have is to be informed, because the more you know, the more in control you'll feel, and the better able you will be to cope with the demands on your body.

Parenting classes also give you valuable baby experience. Visit women from your classes who have their babies before you so that you become familiar with the way a newborn looks and feels.

Planning the birth

If you want your partner to be with you at the birth, ideally he should accompany you to your prenatal classes and practice relaxation and breathing techniques with you. If you prefer not to have a birth partner, of if you would rather have someone other than your partner in the delivery room with you, explain your feelings and decision to your partner to avoid confusion or hurt feelings. It's important that you do whatever feels right for you.

You may already have decided on some aspects of your delivery. For example, you may both feel strongly about having a natural, drug-free birth. Make your health-care provider aware of your desires, and confirm that he or she will follow your wishes if possible. Understand, however, that things don't always work out as planned, and that you may have to compromise your vision of an "ideal birth" because of medical complications or unexpected circumstances.

Practical considerations

Pregnant women are entitled to a number of financial benefits, but some of these have to be applied for at particular times during your pregnancy. Find out about any maternity rights and benefits that you are entitled to early in your pregnancy. If your partner intends taking paternity leave after the birth, he will need to make arrangements with his employers in advance.

If you are planning on returning to work after your baby is born, look into child-care options now. Talk to other mothers about their arrangements and whether they're happy with the child-care services they have. Many day-care centers have long waiting lists, and not all centers accept newborn or very young babies. It's best to sign up with a day care center now—you can change your mind later if you find that your needs have changed.

TAKING A VACATION

If you want to have a last vacation as a "twosome" before the baby arrives, make sure to check the airline's policy on carrying pregnant women. Some airlines do not allow women who are more than 27 weeks pregnant to fly with them because of the risk of them going into premature labor. It's also important to check immunization requirements before you book a trip abroad. Some immunizations, such as a typhoid vaccine, should not be given during pregnancy. Wherever you go, make sure you take your pregnancy record with you in case you need medical treatment while you are away.

Third trimester: weeks 27–40

Your body will now start to undergo even more dramatic changes as it continues to expand to accommodate your growing baby and prepare for the birth. You will be offered a prenatal checkup every two weeks from week 28 to week 36. From then on, you will have a checkup every week until your baby is born.

Pregnancy tests

You may be given a blood test at around 28 weeks to check for anemia. This is caused by an abnormally low level of red blood cells. It's usually treated by taking iron supplements and by including iron-rich foods in your diet. You may also be offered a test for gestational diabetes. You may be given a check for Group B streptococcus (GBS), also known as strep B, at your 36-week checkup.

Common discomforts

Many of the discomforts of the second trimester such as cramp, backache, and edema will continue—and may even become worse. The additional strain your body is under can affect everything from your digestive system to your muscles and joints.

Aches and pains

Relaxin, one of the pregnancy hormones, causes your ligaments to soften in readiness for the birth and results in some aches and pains toward the end of your pregnancy, especially around the pelvic area. In late pregnancy abdominal stretching, sometimes called hot spots, can cause an uncomfortable burning sensation over your abdomen. You may experience sciatica, or lower back and leg pain, as pressure from your enlarging uterus affects the sciatic nerve. Braxton Hicks contractions are likely to become more intense and maybe even painful just before labor begins.

Feeling hot

Because of your body's increased fat deposits and increased metabolism, you will feel much warmer than usual toward the end of your pregnancy. As your baby's birth draws near, you are likely find that you feel very warm most of the time. This is because your circulation is working at maximum efficiency.

Insomnia and fatigue

You may feel incredibly tired but be unable to get a good night's sleep because of physical discomfort, your baby kicking, and frequent trips to the bathroom. When you do get to sleep, you may experience vivid dreams—these are a way of subconsciously sorting out your fears and worries about impending motherhood. If insomnia is getting you down, try to look on it as good practice for the disturbed nights that await you once your baby is born.

Fluid retention

During pregnancy your body swells because of the natural accumulation of fluid in the tissues. Strange at it sounds, you can help to reduce the swelling by drinking plenty of water and by sitting with your feet up whenever you can.

If fluid retention makes your rings tight on your fingers, hold your arms above your head for a minute or two so that the fluid drains downward, relieving the swelling in your fingers. If you have a problem getting your rings off, apply an ice cube, then a drop of dishwashing liquid to your fingers. This will reduce the swelling and lubricate your skin, allowing the rings to slip off easily.

SELF-HELP TIPS

• If your nipples feel sore, leave your breasts exposed to the air for a short while each day when you are relaxing at home.

• Always wear gloves when you are gardening to protect your hands and to keep you free from the risk of toxoplasmosis.

• Help yourself look and feel good by following a nutritious diet and a sensible exercise program throughout your pregnancy.

• Keep your bedroom well humidified during winter months, when heat sources can dry the air.

• Allow plenty of fresh air into your home.

• Living plants improve the air quality around you, so have plants in your home and place of employment.

How your baby grows

By the time you reach your third trimester, your baby—who is now 25 weeks—measures about 10 in (25 cm) from head to foot, and he weighs about 2½ lbs (1.25 kg).

Your baby's development: weeks 25–38

Week 25 Your baby now probably sucks his thumb. This soothes him and also helps to strengthen his cheek and jaw muscles.

Week 26 Hair is starting to grow on your baby's head.

Week 27 Your baby's brain is developing fast and it can now control his breathing and body temperature.

Week 28 As your baby lays down fat he becomes less wrinkled and looks more like a newborn.

Week 29 Your baby's eye color starts to develop. However, your baby's true eye color won't be apparent until six to nine months after the birth.

Week 30 All of your baby's senses are working—he can hear, see, taste, touch, and smell.

Week 31 Your baby produces about 1 pint (600 ml) of urine a day. This is released into the amniotic fluid, and the waste products are filtered through the placenta into your bloodstream. They are then expelled from your body through your kidneys.

Week 32 Even though he can't breathe in air, your baby will practice his breathing movements. The more he develops, the more regular these movements become.

Week 33 Your baby's central nervous system is maturing, his digestive system is almost complete, and his lungs are developed enough to make respiratory problems unlikely. If your baby is born at or after this time, he has a good chance of survival.

Week 34 You will be familiar with your baby's sleeping and waking periods and notice that he is awake for longer periods now.

Week 35 Between now and the birth your baby's weight will increase by about 1 lb (0.5 kg) each week.

Week 36 Your baby's fingers and toenails are fully grown.

Week 37 Mature enough to be born, you can feel your baby's head pressing down on your pelvic floor as he gets ready for birth.

Week 38 To be born your baby has to travel some 9 in (23 cm) down the birth canal into the outside world. At the end of pregnancy, the umbilical cord is about the same length as your baby—about 20 in (51 cm) long.

Preparing for labor

A sudden surge of energy, which often manifests as a "nesting instinct," is quite normal at the end of pregnancy. You may feel the need to redecorate, or to clean your home from top to bottom. Try not to overdo things, as you'll need all your energy for the labor. Pack your hospital bag at least four weeks before your delivery date, leaving room for any last-minute items, just in case your baby decides to arrive early.

Signs to look out for

Your baby will be less active during the last few weeks of pregnancy—she has less room in which to move about. It's important to feel some activity, however, so keep a check on her movements, and report any serious decline to your health-care practitioner. As you approach your due date you will experience some physical changes that indicate that your body is preparing for birth.

Engagement

At around week 36 your uterus will have reached its highest point just under your breastbone. It will move down slightly into the pelvis before the birth—this is sometimes known as the head "engaging" or the "baby dropping." If this is your first baby, this is likely to happen several weeks before the birth, although it can occur as late as the onset of labor.

A show

The mucous plug—a clear, gelatinous blob that has sealed
your cervix throughout your pregnancy—sometimes becomes
dislodged as the cervix begins to dilate. Known as a "show," this
is a sign that your body is preparing for labor, but it doesn't
necessarily mean that it will happen imminently.

Waters breaking

Your water can break before you feel any serious contractions,
but labor usually begins sometime within 24 hours of that event.
You will experience your waters breaking as either a trickle or a
gush of clear, odorless fluid from the vagina.

How your body changes

You can expect to gain 10 to 12 lbs (4.5 to 5.4 kg) during the
third trimester, however, your weight gain is likely to slow down
in the last month, and you may even lose some weight before
labor. Your breasts will produce colostrum (your baby's first food)
during late pregnancy and for the first few days after the birth.

YOUR EMOTIONS

You may excitedly be counting the days to the birth. Remember
that only 5 percent of women deliver on their due date, so be
prepared for your baby not to arrive on time. Alternatively, you
may be anxious about labor and experience prenatal depression.
Talking about your fears should help overcome these feelings.

Your labor and birth experience

Labor is divided into three stages. Knowing what to expect
when each stage occurs will help prepare you for this
amazing event. One of the first signs that your baby is getting
ready to be born is when his head descends into your lower
pelvis. This is known as the head becoming "engaged" or
"dropping". If this is your first baby, this can happen several
weeks before the birth, but in subsequent pregnancies it
often happens as labor begins. Other signs that labor has
begun—or is about to begin—are a "show," rupture of the
membranes, often referred to as the "waters breaking," and
contractions. Early, irregular contractions are sometimes
known as "false labor." These contractions start to soften the
cervix and begin to stretch the lower uterus to allow room for
the baby to move down. When labor begins your cervix will
have thinned out (effaced) and opened up (dilated) to between
2 and 4 cm. Once the contractions become regular, even
though they may be 20 to 30 minutes apart and only last for
20 to 60 seconds, labor has begun.

Early labor

The first stage of labor can last a long time. Unless you are in
extreme discomfort or there is a medical problem, you may find it
easier to experience it at home in familiar surroundings. However,
you must notify your health-care provider if your waters break.

Some women experience a surge of energy during early labor.
No matter how energized you feel, this is not the time to clean
the house or dance around. Try to conserve your strength—you'll
need it during the rest of your labor. To keep up your energy
levels, eat small amounts of easily digested food at frequent

intervals. Avoid foods such as meat and full-fat dairy products that are difficult to digest. It's important to urinate frequently during the first stage, even if you don't feel the need. A full bladder can inhibit the progress of labor.

Prostaglandins, chemicals that are released into a woman's body during early labor, can cause diarrhea and make you shiver and tremble. You may also experience cramps, backache, and an increase in bowel movements during this stage.

Once you begin to have regular contractions, you shouldn't be on your own. You may find it comforting to rest against your partner during each contraction. Or you may prefer to try different labor positions to find the one that is most comfortable for you. Practicing relaxation techniques during contractions can be helpful, but hold off on doing your breathing exercises until you've entered the transitional stage, as they will become boring and tiring if they are used too early. You may find that taking a warm bath or shower will make you feel more comfortable.

As you progress through this first stage your contractions will become stronger and more frequent. These powerful upper uterine contractions gradually push the baby through the stretchable lower uterus. When the contractions come regularly at approximately five-minute intervals and last 45 to 60 seconds each, go to the hospital or birthing center.

When you arrived at the hospital you may offered a wheelchair so that you can be transported to the maternity ward where your condition will be assessed. This is a good time to make sure that your provider is aware of your desired birth plan. However, you should be prepared to compromise or even abandon your birth plan if you or your baby experience complications. Your health and the safe delivery of your baby are all that matters in the end.

Active Labor

Active labor is reached when the cervix begins to dilate rapidly—about 1 cm per hour if you are a first-time mother. During this phase, contractions last for 45 to 60 seconds each, and they become progressively stronger and more frequent. You may find that it helps to move around and change position during contractions. Immersion in water can provide relief from the pain, and it may even help to speed up the labor process. If you find the contractions hard to bear, don't be afraid to ask for pain relief. Even if you had planned to have a natural birth, give yourself permission to change your mind if the contractions become too much to cope with—labor isn't a test of pain endurance. It is important to try to relax between contractions as this will help to conserve your energy for the birth.

The physical effort of labor will increase your breathing rate and your heart rate, and it may cause nausea and sweating. Your blood pressure, breathing, and temperature will be checked throughout your labor and your health-care provider will monitor your baby throughout your labor and delivery.

Unless your health-care provider says otherwise, try to drink plenty of cool liquids to prevent dehydration. If your doctor doesn't want you to drink liquids, ask if you can suck on some ice cubes instead.

Some hospitals follow a policy of "active management of labor" (AMOL) for first-time labors. In accordance with this policy, if your labor doesn't proceed within a certain time frame, your health-care provider will intervene to help it along. Don't be afraid to ask your health-care provider to explain anything that you don't understand or are concerned about.

Transitional labor

Transitional labor is the most difficult and demanding period,
during which the cervix fully dilates from 8 to 10 cm. Contractions
will now occur at two to three minute intervals and last between
60 and 90 seconds. Try to remember when you get to the transition
phase that the end is in sight—the stronger the contractions, the
nearer you are to giving birth. Labor is so-called because it is hard
work so view your contractions as work rather than as pain. Work
with your body, and try to focus on the goal you are aiming for—
the safe delivery of your baby. Don't be embarrassed if you make
a lot of noise during this time, most women lose their inhibitions
during labor.

Don't panic during contractions, or you may "over-breathe,"
which can cause hyperventilation. Take deep, slow breaths at
the beginning and end of each contraction to ensure the
maximum delivery of oxygen to your own system and to your
baby. Muscles that are deprived of oxygen produce lactic acid,
and an accumulation of this acid causes pain. This is one reason
why it is very important to breathe correctly during labor.

Use strategies such as breathing techniques, massage,
meditation, and imaging to distract you from the physical discomfort
your body is experiencing. Relaxation techniques will help prevent
your muscles from tensing. Relaxed muscles make it easier for your
uterus to stretch as your baby passes through your pelvis.

Upright positions can shorten labor, as gravity helps to speed
up your baby's descent. By shifting position, you can help guide
your baby through the curvature of your lower abdomen and
pelvis. But if you find it more comfortable to lie down, lie on your
side and support your body well with cushions. Labor is
sometimes slowed when a woman lies on her back.

As you reach the period before the birth, you may experience a lull in your contractions before pushing begins and you may experience a renewed burst of energy. This second stage of labor usually takes about an hour, but it can last as little as ten minutes or as long as three hours. During this stage, contractions usually last for 60 to 90 seconds each and occur at two to four minute intervals. Concentrate on each contraction as it happens. Stay focused on what is happening in the moment; don't think about what has happened or what may be to come.

The pushing stage

The feeling of wanting to bear down or push usually occurs between two and fours times within the course of a contraction, but it is sometimes felt as one long, continuous urge. The length of the push isn't as important as is pushing with the contraction. You may experience an overwhelming urge to push your baby out, but you will need to wait until your health-care provider says that it is all right to do so. The perineum should thin from about 5 cm in thickness to less than 1 cm during the birth. Controlled pushing will allow it to stretch gradually, which will help prevent tears or the need for an episiotomy—a surgical cut in the perineum. To help slow things down, try panting. Try to be as upright as possible when pushing so that you are working with gravity rather than against it.

During the pushing stage your baby is actively helping himself to be born by pushing away from the uterus wall with his feet and by wriggling his head through your cervix and vagina. Your baby's skull bones are soft, and they are designed to overlap so that his head becomes smaller as it is pushed down your vagina. Your baby's head has "crowned" when the widest part of it can be seen at the vaginal opening. Reach down and touch your baby's head once it has crowned. This will give you encouragement to keep going when it gets tough to push. If you want to watch your baby being born, ask someone to hold a mirror so that you can easily see the progress you are making.

Birth

As your baby's head is being born you will feel pressure on your rectum and a burning, stinging sensation around your vagina. As your baby's head pushes its way out through the vagina, the pressure it puts on the nerves in this area naturally numbs the perineum. Your baby will usually be born with her head face down. After her head comes out of the birth canal, she will turn it to one side, and her shoulders will come out one at a time. They are followed immediately by the rest of her body. She will be given to you to hold a few minutes later. You may want your partner to cut the umbilical cord once your baby is born. The cord will be clamped in two places and cut between the clamped sections.

Occasionally a baby needs help being delivered. If this occurs, you will be given a regional anesthetic (if you have not already had an epidural or a spinal block) to prevent your discomfort, and vacuum extraction or forceps will be used to ease the head out.

Birth of the placenta

The third stage of labor—the birth of the placenta—usually lasts from five minutes to half an hour and should cause you little discomfort.Your may be offered an injection of syntometrine to speed up the delivery of the placenta and to reduce any postpartum bleeding. If you wish to deliver the placenta naturally, you may be encouraged to breast-feed as nipple stimulation naturally releases oxytocin, the hormone that promotes uterine contractions. Your health-care provider may massage your uterus and gently pull on the umbilical cord as you push the placenta out.

Once the placenta has been expelled from the uterus it will be examined to check that it is whole and that nothing has been left behind. If anything has been left in the uterus, it will be removed manually. The placenta weighs about 1 lb (0.5 kg) at the time of your baby's birth.

If you require stitches, you will be given a local injection in the perineum to numb the area, and the procedure shouldn't hurt. If you don't need stitches, your perineum may still be sore so ask your health-care provider for an ice pack as this will help soothe the area.

After you've given birth

It's natural to feel a range of emotions right after the birth of your baby. Your strongest feelings will probably be excitement about meeting your child for the first time and relief that the delivery is safely over. You may bond with your newborn immediately, or you may find that you feel rather detached from your baby, especially if you have had a difficult delivery. Don't be concerned; you and your baby will soon learn to love each other. Start the bonding process by talking to your baby while you hold and cuddle her. She will already know your voice from hearing it while she was in the uterus. Hearing it in her strange new environment will give her comfort.

Don't expect your baby to look like the round, rosy-cheeked cherub you see in pictures. Nine months in amniotic fluid, along with the tight squeeze through the birth canal, will have taken their temporary toll on your baby's appearance. Your baby's head may look slightly pointed immediately after the birth but within a week or two it will have lost this shape and have become rounded.

Rest assured that this "newborn look" won't last for more than a few weeks. Your newborn may have a covering of fine downy hair on his back and shoulders, and perhaps even on his forehead and temples. This will quickly disappear, usually within a week of the birth. If your baby arrives prematurely, he's likely to still be covered in vernix, a greasy substance that has protected his skin from becoming waterlogged by amniotic fluid. Don't be alarmed—this will soon wear off.

What happens to your baby

Your baby is likely to be placed on your abdomen as soon as she is born. The familiar sound of your heartbeat will comfort her as she spends her first moments in her strange new world. Once the umbilical cord has been cut your baby's nose and mouth will be suctioned to remove excess mucus. This is a standard procedure, and it's nothing to worry about.

Your baby's first test will be the Apgar score. This checks for appearance and color, pulse, reflex, activity, and respiration. Your baby will be tested for these one minute after her birth, and again five minutes later. A score of six and above is fine; anything less may mean that the baby needs some help.

Having a cesarean section

A cesarean section involves major abdominal surgery and is only proposed if you and/or your baby are considered to be at risk. After a cesarean you will have to remain in hospital for longer than if you'd had a vaginal delivery.

Elective cesarean

This is planned in advance and usually takes place before labor has started. The most common reason for an elective cesarean is having had a previous cesarean. A planned cesarean may also be suggested if you are pregnant with more than one baby; if your baby is thought to be too big to fit easily through your pelvis, or your baby is lying in the wrong position in the uterus. Other reasons include medical problems affecting either the mother or the baby.

You will either be given a "regional" anesthetic which means the abdominal area is anesthetized and you remain awake, or a "general" where you are unconscious during the operation. Your partner can usually stay with you if you remain conscious during the operation.

Advanced planning can make an elective cesarean a more satisfying experience. Go to childbirth classes that include information on cesareans and visit your hospital's labor and childbirth areas so that you are familiar with the type of room where you will have your baby.

Emergency cesarean

An emergency cesarean is carried out as a result of a complication that occurs once labor has begun. The baby may be distressed or mother and baby may be too exhausted to proceed with a vaginal delivery. A general anesthetic is usually given so that the baby can be born as quickly as possible.

If you have to have an emergency cesarean, make sure that you and your partner understand the reasons for the operation. If there's no time beforehand, ask the questions afterwards, before you leave the hospital.

Coping with health issues

Digestive problems

During pregnancy you are likely to experience a number of health problems which can vary from being annoying to extremely uncomfortable. Many pregnancy problems can be reduced or even prevented by simple self-help measures, but if you are concerned, always consult your health-care professionals. Sometimes symptoms are a sign of something more serious which requires immediate medical attention. The most common problems you are likely to experience during your pregnancy are to do with your digestive system. Pregnancy hormones cause nausea and slow down digestion which can result in a number of unpleasant side effects.

Constipation

Some of the extra hormones produced during pregnancy relax the intestines, which become sluggish and less efficient. This can cause constipation. Be sure to eat plenty of vegetables, fruits, and other foods that are high in fiber every day to help keep your intestines in good working order. Drinking plenty of fluids will help prevent constipation by keeping food moving along the digestive tract. Fluids also help to keep your stools soft. Taking regular exercise will encourage bowel activity, so make time for a brisk 20-minute walk each day.

It's also important not to rush things when you're on the toilet, so always allow yourself plenty of time to empty your bowels. You may find that it helps to completely relax your pelvic floor muscles. To do this, pull the muscles up as tightly as you can, then let them relax.

Gas

Pregnant women burp, and they pass gas. These conditions are inescapable—they're just part of being pregnant. Although you can't prevent them, you can avoid making them worse by refraining from overeating and by avoiding constipation. Some women who suffer from excessive gas find some relief by cutting out fried foods, rich foods, onions, and cabbage from their diets.

Morning sickness

Although morning sickness can occur at any time of the day, many women do experience it first thing in the morning. It can vary in intensity, producing symptoms that range from slight nausea to actual vomiting. You may experience morning sickness as soon as five weeks into your pregnancy. From about the twelfth week on, however, it usually become less frequent or disappears all together—although a few women are unfortunate enough to suffer from it throughout the nine months.

Morning sickness tends to occur when your stomach is empty so you can help relieve the symptoms early in the day by having a dry cracker and a cup of ginger tea before getting up. Eating small meals that contain easy-to-digest carbohydrates, such as potatoes or dry toast, throughout the day and sucking on a lemon, or drinking the juice mixed with hot water will all help relieve feelings of nausea and sickness.

If your morning sickness is severe and you find that you can't keep anything down, or if you experience weight loss, notify your doctor. He or she will want to rule out hyperemesis gravidarum, a more severe form of vomiting in pregnancy that may require medical treatment.

Heartburn

The high levels of progesterone produced by your body during pregnancy can slow digestion and relax the sphincter muscle that connects the esophagus to the stomach, causing heartburn which can be very uncomfortable. You can help prevent heartburn by eating small, frequent meals and by avoiding spicy, fatty, and greasy foods, and by not eating too close to bedtime.

Heartburn can be relieved by sitting upright and eating a dry cracker as this will help to neutralize the acid that causes heartburn pain. Antacids can also help, but make sure that they are suitable for use during pregnancy before you take one, and don't exceed the recommended dosage.

LOOSE STOOLS

If you suffer from loose stools, try cutting back on bowel-stimulating foods, such as dried fruit, and drink plenty of fluids.

Aches, pains, and itches

Pregnancy puts your body under a great deal of strain so it's natural to suffer some aches and pains, especially during the latter months when your growing bump affects your balance and posture. High levels of pregnancy hormones can also cause other health concerns.

Headaches

Pregnancy headaches are often caused by hormonal changes. Since it's best not to take pain relievers while you're pregnant (unless prescribed by your doctor) you need to find other ways of overcoming or preventing them. Relaxation techniques, such as yoga and meditation, will help, as will an ice pack applied to the back of the neck. Headaches that are brought on by fatigue or hunger can be prevented by getting plenty of rest and eating regularly. Heated, stuffy rooms may cause your head to ache, so avoid them, or if that's not possible, take frequent breathers in the fresh air. Be careful not to sit hunched over your work or a book, as poor posture can cause headaches.

If you suffer from sinus headaches, try applying hot and cold compresses to the area, alternating them at 30-second intervals for at least 10 minutes.

If you have a particularly persistent headache or one accompanied by blurred vision or puffiness in your hands and feet, flashing lights in front of your eyes, and double vision, contact your doctor at once, as this could be a sign of pre-eclampsia.

Cramps

No one knows for certain what causes leg cramps during pregnancy, although they have been linked to low levels of magnesium or calcium. Leg cramps are sometimes thought to be caused by a combination of fatigue and the buildup of fluid that has accumulated in the legs during the day. To help ease the pain, walk around the room in bare feet, and stretch and massage the affected muscle.

Cramping during and after orgasm is very common and harmless during a normal pregnancy, and it is not a sign that sex is hurting your baby.

RESTLESS LEG SYNDROME

Restless leg syndrome is experienced by about 15 percent of pregnant women. The syndrome is marked by a restless, tingling feeling inside the foot or leg. Although it can occur at any time, women often experience it at night. No one is sure of the cause, and there is no proven treatment for it.

Round ligament pain

During pregnancy the round ligaments, bands of fibrous tissue on each side of the uterus, stretch, and can cause a sharp pain or a dull ache on one or both sides of your lower abdomen, near your groin, between weeks 18 and 24. To help relieve this, keep off your feet as much as you can, and sit with your feet up. Round ligament pain usually goes away after week 24.

Back pain

As you become bigger, your ligaments and joints begin to relax in preparation for the birth. This can cause your body to become unbalanced, which in turn can cause back pain. Pressure from the enlarged uterus can also affect the sciatic nerve, causing pain in the lower back, buttocks, and legs. A heating pad, applied locally for short periods of time, may help, as will rest. Swimming can sometimes relieve pressure on the sciatic nerve.

You can help to prevent backache by adjusting your posture so that you are carrying your weight evenly when you walk or stand. Always make sure your back is well supported when you are sitting, and place your feet on a low footstool so that your knees are level with your hips. Be sure to bend your knees before lifting anything up off the ground. When carrying shopping bags, divide the weight evenly and carry a bag in each hand. Sleep on a firm mattress that supports your back and give yourself extra support by putting a pillow between your knees and under your belly when you lie on your side.

Symphysis pubis dysfunction

This occurs as a mild to severe pain in the pubic area and is caused by pregnancy hormones. Symphysis pubis dysfunction can occur any time from the end of the first trimester. The condition is untreatable, but your health-care provider may be able to suggest some exercises that may help to relieve the pain.

Swelling

The increased amount of fluids in your body can cause swelling, particularly in the hands and feet. Try drinking plenty of liquids to help expel excess fluid. Reduce the swelling in your hands by elevating them above your heart.

Numbness and tingling

Swelling tissues pressing on the nerves are thought to be the cause of numbness and tingling in the fingers and toes during pregnancy. If you experience numbness and pain in your thumb, index finger, and middle finger (and, sometimes, in your wrist), with pain radiating up your arm, you might have pregnancy-related carpal tunnel syndrome. Your health-care provider may recommend a wrist splint. Pregnancy-related carpal tunnel syndrome usually goes away two to three weeks after the birth.

Breast discomfort

Increased amounts of estrogen and progesterone in your body cause your breasts to feel tender and swollen. Although the feeling of tenderness should subside or disappear after the fourth month, make sure that your breasts are well supported throughout your entire pregnancy. Hormonal changes may cause nipples to become sore. Soothe them with baby oil or a specially formulated nipple cream.

Hemorrhoids

These are varicose veins in the rectum, which are caused by the uterus pressing on major blood vessels. Hemorrhoids can be very painful. Some women find relief by putting witch hazel on them and by sitting on a cooling gel pad, or your doctor can prescribe a soothing ointment for them.

Anal fissures

These small tears in the lining of the anus are often caused by constipation and are fairly common during pregnancy. They can be very painful, especially if they are accompanied by hemorrhoids. To help prevent anal fissures, try to avoid constipation, and keep the perineal area scrupulously clean. Notify your doctor immediately if you experience any rectal bleeding.

Urinary tract infections

Urinary tract infections such as cystitis are quite common in pregnancy. If you experience pain when urinating, or if you have blood-tinged urine, you may have a urinary tract infection which will require medical treatment.

Vaginal infections

If you experience severe itching around your vulva and your vagina is red, sore, and burning, you probably have thrush, a yeast infection that is very common in pregnant women. A mild attack of thrush may require only a change of diet. Try cutting out sugar and white flour, and replacing them with whole grains, fruits, vegetables, and protein. You can try treating thrush naturally by adding four drops of tea tree oil to a bowl of warm water or a sitz bath and sitting in it for five to ten minutes. Make sure you keep the genital area clean and dry and avoid using scented soaps, bubble bath, and talcum powder, which can cause further irritation. If the attack is severe, consult your doctor. He or she can prescribe a vaginal suppository that is safe for you to use during pregnancy. Once you contract thrush, you are likely to find that it recurs quite frequently throughout the rest of your pregnancy.

Itching

Because your metabolic rate increases during pregnancy and there is more blood circulating throughout your body, you will sweat more than usual. This is likely to cause rashes where the skin creases—for example, in the groin and under the breasts. To help stay cool shower frequently, using warm (not hot) water and a soap-free cleanser. Avoid using soap too often, as it can make the skin dry. Always towel dry the skin thoroughly afterwards and wear natural materials, such as cotton, that allow your skin to breathe. You can soothe this itching with calamine lotion or moisturizing creams. If you suffer from severe itching, especially during the last weeks of your pregnancy, seek urgent medical attention. This could be a sign of a rare but dangerous liver disease called choleostasis. Other symptoms of choleostasis include jaundice, dark urine, and a general feeling of being unwell.

Other concerns

Your body is having to work very hard as your baby grows and as a direct result of all the changes that are taking place you may experience a number of common—or occasionally not so common—complaints as your pregnancy progresses.

Fatigue

It is perfectly normal to feel exhausted during the first trimester, when so many physical changes are taking place. This feeling should lessen around weeks 12 to 14 and you'll start feeling more energetic again, and more like your normal self. Toward the end of your pregnancy you will feel tired because of all the extra weight you are carrying, and because your sleep is being disturbed by numerous trips to the bathroom during the night. It's important to get as much rest as you can, and to be realistic about what you can do without becoming exhausted.

Other factors, such as inadequate lighting, poor air circulation or quality, and excessive noise in your home or workplace can make you feel tired, so be aware of such problems in your surroundings, and correct them whenever possible.

Don't rely on caffeine or sweets to give you a quick energy lift. They will only leave your body feeling more fatigued as soon as your blood-sugar level drops. Remember to take plenty of exercise during the first and second trimesters as too much rest and not enough physical activity can make fatigue worse.

Dizziness

At the beginning of pregnancy you may experience dizziness because your blood flow is struggling to keep up with your increased circulation. Later in pregnancy dizziness may be the result of the uterus pressing on large blood vessels. If you feel faint, put your head down between your knees, or lie down for a few minutes with your feet higher than your head. These positions will increase the circulation of blood to your brain. Dizziness can also occur when you sit up or stand up too quickly, so always get up slowly from sitting or lying positions.

Low blood-sugar levels can lead to dizziness so eat small, frequent meals that are rich in protein, and carry a snack of raisins or crackers in your bag in case you require a quick blood-sugar lift. Dizziness may also be a sign of dehydration so keep up your intake of liquids.

Nasal congestion

The increased blood flow throughout your body can cause the lining of your nasal passages to become swollen. This can lead to congestion and an overproduction of mucus. Help clear nasal congestion by increasing your fluid intake, humidifying your home (especially your bedroom), and sleeping propped up at night. You can make yourself more comfortable by taking frequent sips of water to prevent your mouth from becoming dry, and use a lip salve to prevent your lips from becoming sore.

If you suffer from severe congestion, cover your head with a towel and hold it over a bowl of hot water for five to ten minutes, breathing in the steam. Avoid congestion medication or nasal sprays unless they have prescribed by your health-care provider.

Poor concentration

The loss of concentration that occurs during pregnancy is quite normal and is caused by hormonal changes. Try to keep stress to a minimum, and accept that forgetfulness is part of your life until after the baby is born.

Breathlessness

You may find that you become short of breath as your pregnancy progresses and your enlarged uterus starts to press against your diaphragm and lungs. Any form of exertion may make you feel breathless. Although this may be alarming, try not to panic, as that will only make you feel worse. When you feel breathless, stand or sit up straight so that your chest has plenty of room to expand. Any feelings of breathlessness will lessen in the final weeks of your pregnancy, as your baby moves down into your pelvis.

Severe breathlessness, marked by rapid breathing and a slight, bluish discoloration of the lips and fingertips, may be a sign of trouble, especially if accompanied by chest pain. Contact your health care provider immediately if you experience this.

NONFOOD CRAVINGS

Pregnant women may develop a rare condition known as pica. This is marked by a compulsion to eat nonfood substances such as coal, chalk, toothpaste, or burned matches. Pica can interfere with the absorption of essential minerals, and it may also reduce a woman's intake of nutritious foods. For these reasons, always discuss any nonfood craving with your health-care professional.

Anemia

Iron-deficiency anemia can make you feel drained, dizzy, faint, and short of breath. Your doctor may treat the anemia with a prescribed supplement, and you may be told to increase your intake of iron-rich foods such as red meat, beans, and spinach.

Increased saliva

During the early weeks of pregnancy you may experience an increase in the amount of saliva you produce and notice that it has a bitter taste. This excessive salivation is an unusual complication of pregnancy known as ptyalism. To help reduce the saliva that's produced, cut down on starchy foods and dairy products, and eat plenty of fruit. Mints and chewing gum can help reduce saliva production, and mint-flavored toothpaste and dental floss will help freshen your mouth. Although the cause is unknown, you are more likely to suffer from it if you have morning sickness. Ptyalism generally clears up spontaneously—usually by the third trimester.

Frequent urination

At the beginning of your pregnancy you will find that you need to urinate frequently. This is because of the additional body fluid that your kidneys are having to process, and because the growing uterus is pressing on your bladder. Don't be tempted to cut down on fluids in an effort to urinate less as this will only make the problem worse and may also cause dehydration. Drink eight glasses of water a day and practice pulling up your pelvic floor muscles to control your bladder and always go as soon as you feel the urge.

During the last months of pregnancy you may find that you leak small amounts of urine when you cough, sneeze, or laugh.

Increase the number of Kegel exercises that you do each day to strengthen the muscles that support the urinary sphincter, which are the muscles that keeps the bladder closed.

Once your baby has moved down into your pelvis, during the last few weeks of your pregnancy, your need to urinate will become even more frequent, and you may find that it prevents you from getting a good night's sleep. Lean forward when you urinate to help the bladder completely empty as this will reduce the number of trips you have to make to the bathroom.

Increased vaginal discharge

A thin, white, mild-smelling discharge is normal throughout pregnancy. Although it begins lightly, it increases as your pregnancy progresses. You may feel more comfortable wearing disposable panty liners that will absorb the discharge. Don't use tampons, as these can introduce unwanted germs into the vagina and cause infection.

Varicose veins

These are swollen veins that appear under the surface of the skin of your legs. You are more likely to get them if they run in your family, if you are overweight, or if you spend a lot of time standing or sitting. Although varicose veins are usually painless, they are unsightly, and even though they will shrink after the birth, they often don't disappear completely. Minimize the chance of getting them by avoiding long periods of standing and by taking rest periods with your feet up. Alternatively, if you have to sit for long periods, you can help prevent varicose veins by moving your legs around from time to time and by flexing your feet. Wearing support stockings will lessen the risk of them developing in the first place.

Gestational diabetes

If you have had gestational diabetes before, you're over 35, overweight, or Asian, or if your previous baby was over 8 lbs, 13 oz (4 kg) or you have a parent or a sibling with diabetes, there is a risk of developing gestational diabetes. Your blood sugar levels will be checked regularly for signs of the disease.

If you are a diabetic you will need to control your sugar levels both before and during pregnancy to increase the chance of your baby developing normally.

Pre-eclampsia

Pre-eclampsia affects about between 5 and 8 per cent of pregnancies and can develop anytime after 20 weeks. If you had high blood pressure before you became pregnant, you're a first time or teenage mother, or you are carrying more than one baby, there is an increased risk of your developing pre-eclampsia. If pre-eclampsia is suspected, your health-care provider will want to monitor you very closely and you will need to eat a low-fat diet and get plenty of rest and relaxation. If it occurs after week 37 of pregnancy, labor is likely to be induced.

Rarely, pre-eclampsia leads to eclampsia, which is a very serious condition. Symptoms include seizures and possible coma. If you develop this, your baby will need to be delivered immediately.

Alternative therapies

As pregnancy is a natural state, many women believe that alternative and complementary therapies have a part to play in helping them through this stage of their lives. However, it's important to remember that even if something is "natural," it's not necessarily safe for you to use during pregnancy so you should always consult your health-care provider before embarking on any form of treatment. Therapies such as homeopathy and herbalism are often used as alternatives to conventional medicine. Practitioners believe that illness is caused by a disruption of physical and mental well being. Treatment, which should always be used with caution during pregnancy, involves stimulating the body's natural self-healing abilities.

Homeopathic remedies

The goal of homeopathy—a holistic form of medicine that aims to help the body heal itself—is to treat the whole person, not just the person's symptoms. Homeopathic remedies treat like with like, in minute quantities. The majority of remedies are derived from plants, but some are derived from mineral sources, and others come from animals. Many remedies are safe for use in pregnancy, but it can be difficult to decide on the correct homeopathic remedy for a particular ailment, so never self-prescribe. Always seek advice from a qualified homeopath and check with your doctor before taking the remedies.

Homeopathy can be effective in the treatment of minor complaints such as morning sickness, heartburn, and nausea.

Herbal remedies

Herbal medicines are not tested in the same way as conventional drugs are, so their safety and effectiveness haven't been clinically established. For this reason, and because some herbs are extremely potent—for example, ginkgo biloba should never be taken during pregnancy—some health-care providers do not recommend their use during pregnancy. If your doctor agrees to their use, you should seek the guidance of a qualified herbal practitioner.

Arnica

Arnica is sometimes taken as a tincture diluted in water a week before a woman's due date to help prevent bruising from labor.

Ginger

Well known for its anti-nausea properties, ginger can be used to reduce nausea and morning sickness, but it should be avoided if you have a peptic ulcer.

Raspberry-leaf tea

Raspberry leaves are thought to tone the uterine muscles, and your homeopathic practitioner may suggest that you take raspberry-leaf tea during the last weeks of your pregnancy. This should never be taken during the first trimester.

Nettle-leaf tea

Nettle leaves are rich in iron, and an infusion made with the leaves and boiling water may be taken throughout pregnancy.

Cloves and sage

These herbs, which are often used in cooking, are both good prenatal "tonics" and can be included in your diet during the last few weeks of your pregnancy.

Complementary therapies

Many complementary therapies are helpful during pregnancy as they relieve stress and boost the body's immune system. If you want a complementary practitioner, such as a reflexologist to attend to you during labor, you will need to check the hospital's policy regarding complementary therapies beforehand.

Essential oils

Although some aromatherapy oils are suitable for use during pregnancy, others are known to be hazardous so it's important to consult your doctor before using products containing plant or herbal oils.

Over-the-counter aromatherapy oils may not be safe for use during pregnancy, so look for specially formulated "prenatal blends" of essential oils or ask a qualified aromatherapist to prescribe a blend for you. Never take essential oils internally or apply them directly onto your skin, unless directed to by a qualified practitioner.

Unless you're trying to induce labor, avoid oils that contain basil, cedarwood, clary sage, fennel, juniper, marjoram, myrrh, rosemary, sage, and thyme, as these are known to stimulate uterine contractions.

Soothing remedies

Once you are past the first trimester, try placing four drops
of essential oil on a cloth on your shower head, so that they
evaporate into the steam when you turn on the water. Two drops
of essential oil of lemon and two drops of essential oil of
geranium will refresh you and balance your emotions.

You can overcome nervous anxiety by placing two drops of
essential oil of ylang-ylang and four drops of essential oil of
geranium onto a tissue then inhale as needed throughout the day.

During the second and third trimesters, soothe and
rebalance your emotions by placing two drops of lavender and
two of geranium essential oils into a quarter cup of milk and
adding it to your bathwater.

Sore breasts can be made more comfortable by adding two
drops of essential oil of lavender or essential oil of geranium to
your bathwater. Relax in the tub, allowing the water to cover
your breasts.

Preparing the perineum

During the last eight weeks of pregnancy, massage the perineum
with a teaspoon of a carrier oil, such as jojoba oil, which has
excellent lubrication properties. This will help the skin to become
supple, and it may prevent tearing during the birth.

Labor

Neroli oil and sandalwood oil can be placed in a vaporizer and
released into the air to soothe you during labor. If your
contractions stop when you are in labor, a few drops of clary
sage, inhaled from a handkerchief, may get them going again.

Bodywork therapies

These "hands-on" treatments can be used effectively to help overcome common pregnancy complaints such as nausea and backache and to assist you through labor. Any treatment must be carried out by a qualified practitioner, with the agreement of your health-care provider.

Acupressure and acupuncture

Both acupressure and acupuncture can be used to relieve pain by releasing endorphins, the body's own painkillers. In acupuncture, very fine needles are used to stimulate the "qi," or energy channels, of the body where ailments may have caused an imbalance. Sometimes moxa herbs are also burnt to create heat to stimulate certain acupuncture points on the body.

Acupressure can be carried out by a therapist who puts pressure on the specific pressure points on the body, that relate to a particular illness. For morning sickness you can take a do-it-yourself approach by wearing acupressure bands, which are readily available in pharmacies and supermarkets. These fit round your wrists and put pressure on the pressure points that relate to nausea.

Biofeedback

This therapy can be used to help you control your responses to pain and emotional stress. It may relieve a number of discomforts that are the result of pregnancy, such as headaches and insomnia.

HYDROTHERAPY

Warm (not hot) water is frequently used to help relax women during labor. Some women choose to give birth immersed in warm water.

Massage

Massage produces endorphins, the body's natural feel-good hormones and can be used throughout pregnancy, providing certain precautions are taken. For example, pressure points that are located near the ankles should be avoided, as these correspond to the ovaries and uterus. Deep pressure applied to this area could bring on premature labor.

You can be massaged, either by your partner or a friend, have a professional massage, or massage yourself. Self-massage is very calming, is good for your muscles, and is a great way to get in touch with your body.

During labor, massage can ease the pain of contractions. Have your birth partner learn the correct techniques, and make sure that he or she knows to follow your direction and your wishes when labor begins. Pressure applied to the lower back and buttocks is often the most effective way to relieve labor pains.

Osteopathic treatments

An osteopath can help you adopt a posture that will relieve backache and prevent sciatica as your pregnancy progresses. Osteopathy can help to relieve digestive problems and constipation.

Chiropractic medicine

Physical manipulation can be used during pregnancy to heal and relieve muscle and joint problems. Make sure that your chiropractor is qualified to treat pregnant women.

Reflexology

Reflexology uses pressure points on your hands or feet that correspond with various areas and organs throughout your body. The use of gentle pressure on these points promotes deep relaxation which encourages the body's healing processes. Reflexology can help relieve a number of common complaints, such as morning sickness and cramp. Although it can be used to reduce the pain of contractions, it can also trigger unwanted contractions if it is used on some pressure points. Always ensure that your reflexologist has been trained in the care of pregnant women. Reflexology may be used to induce labor once you have passed your due date.

Reiki

The natural healing energy involved in Reiki—a form of Japanese spiritual healing—works not only on your physical body, but on every level of your psyche and spirit as well. Reiki promotes the body's regenerative self-healing ability. It will help you respond more calmly to all events, and combat illness and fatigue.

Shiatsu

This is a type of massage that uses finger pressure and is suitable for all stages of pregnancy. It can help relieve constipation, leg cramps, hemorrhoids, nausea, frequent urination, swollen ankles, and fatigue.

Mind therapies

Hypnosis, meditation, and visualization are all known to be useful aids for pregnancy and labor. These techniques have to be learnt, so it's important to find a practitioner that you are in tune with and to start attending classes early on in your pregnancy.

Hypnosis

During the first trimester, a hypnotist may help you overcome some common pregnancy discomforts. If you plan to use self-hypnosis as a method of relieving pain during labor, you need to begin your training months ahead of your due date in order to learn how to do this properly and effectively.

Seek out a trained professional who is certified in the method of teaching self-hypnosis. Do not attempt to learn this from someone who is not qualified to instruct you in self-hypnosis.

Meditation and visualization

Both meditation and visualization can be useful during pregnancy and labor, especially when they are used in conjunction with other relaxation techniques.

Meditation can help to reduce muscle tension, lower your blood pressure, and stimulate relaxation-related alpha brain waves. There is no "correct" way to meditate. Experiment with different methods to find the one that suits you. By practicing this regularly, you can develop the ability to reap the benefits of meditation whenever you feel the need to.

Visualization aids relaxation and will help concentration during labor. Practice visualizing a scene that makes you happy and relaxed—perhaps waves washing onto a soft, white, sandy beach that is edged with palm trees, or a happy event from the past. Once the scene is firmly implanted in your mind, you will be easily able to "put yourself in that happy place" whenever you want to.

SELF-HELP REMEDIES

• Rub vitamin E oil into the skin to help stretch marks from becoming too unsightly.

• Place orange-flower water in an atomizer, and use it to spritz your face when you're feeling warm.

• For a truly relaxing bath, place some loose lavender and chamomile in a muslin bag and tie it to the bath faucet so that the water rushes over it when you fill the tub.

• Tune into music to relax your mind and your body. Scientists believe that certain kinds produce mood-altering chemicals. Try classical and baroque music that feature approximately one beat per second to harmonize the body and brain.

• Soothe yourself with a CD of nature sounds, such as whale songs, waves crashing onto the shore, or thunderstorms.

• Give yourself a quick pick-me-up by standing under the shower for 10 minutes, turning the water from warm to cool and back again as it sprays against your neck and shoulders.

• Focus your awareness on your breathing to help keep yourself calm during stressful situations. Breathing well is the key to health and peace of mind.

Life
with your
new baby

At home with baby

With the arrival of your darling new baby you will find yourself catapulted into a whole new existence of seemingly non-stop tasks and routines that can, at first, seem rather daunting. Being aware of your baby's needs and having the practical knowledge to deal with them will help remove much unnecessary stress. The following pages will arm you with dozens of tips and strategies to help transform everyday mundane jobs, from changing diapers to dressing your baby and looking after him when he's unwell, into opportunities for playing, learning, and deepening the trust between you, helping you and your baby to forge an ever closer bond.

Diaper changing

What should be a straightforward job can all too frequently end in tears as your baby screams his protest at being undressed and exposed to the cold air. But with some forward planning and simple diversion techniques, it's surprisingly easy to transform this potential source of conflict into a fun and effortless task! Turn to page 72 for help on deciding whether to use cloth or disposable diapers.

Make it fun

Keep diaper-changing time fluster-free by gathering together everything you need before you begin, as the more organized you are the less time your baby will have to get really distressed. A good ploy is to have all the essential diaper-changing equipment and a ready-packed diaper bag (for out-of-house excursions) at a designated changing table or area at home.

As well as being efficient, try distracting your baby and make diaper-changing time a social occasion by giving him a running commentary while you change him. Even better, turn it into a game by singing to your baby, tickling his feet, and blowing raspberries on his tummy. He will be delighted, and may forget all about the task at hand.

Keeping your baby comfortable

You can avoid a nasty diaper rash—caused by the ammonia that's released as bacteria in feces breaking down urine—by changing your baby's diapers frequently. This can be every one to two hours in the early months! Warm water and cotton balls are the gentlest tools to use to clean your baby's bottom, especially if he has a sore rash. Apply barrier creams, such as zinc and castor oil or petroleum jelly, to prevent a rash developing or to clear up an existing rash. Baby wipes are convenient, but they can be harsh on your baby's soft skin, so try to limit their use to when you're in a rush or are changing your baby's diaper away from home. Likewise, avoid using talcum powder on your baby, as it could irritate his baby-soft skin.

Give your baby some time each day to roll around naked as he will love the freedom to kick his legs around, and the air on his skin will help to clear up any diaper rash he may have. Further add to his comfort by putting a folded towel over the diaper mat to ensure that he feels comfortable, warm, and relaxed during each change and make sure that the room where you change your baby is warm and draft-free.

Washing and bathing

Bathing your newborn can be a nervewracking experience, but with practice you will quickly build up your confidence. Whether it's a quick clean with cotton wool or bathing him in the big bath, here are plenty of suggestions for trouble-free bathing.

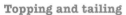

Topping and tailing

If your small baby hates the bath, don't feel pressured into giving him a bath each day. Some experts even believe that daily baths prevent babies from building up their immunity to germs, which may result in allergies. Try alternating bathing with "topping and tailing". Use cooled boiled water and cotton ball pieces to clean his face, behind his ears, his armpits, and his bottom. You can avoid undressing him completely when you clean him by washing his bottom while his top is on, putting on a new diaper, and then removing his top to wash his armpits, hands, and face.

Bathtime

Once your baby starts on solids there will be a lot more mess, and a daily bath will be a good idea. You can build this into his nighttime routine to help him wind down before bedtime. Build your confidence by using a baby bath at first, so that you get used to handling him in water without worrying that he will slip from your grasp. You can ensure the move to the big bath is stress-free by using a specially designed bath support to keep your baby secure and stop him from slipping. Test the bath water temperature by dipping your elbow in. If it feels nicely warm, but not hot, it's ready for your baby. Also, it may seem obvious, but remember that your baby will enjoy bath time more if the room is warm and free from chilly drafts.

A nonslip rubber mat in the big bath will keep your baby safe, and it will help you both to relax at bath time. Most importantly, don't be tempted to leave your baby alone in the bath for even a moment, as accidents can happen quickly, so get together everything you need before you put him in the bath, and ignore the phone and the doorbell.

Hair washing

This can be particularly distressing for your new baby but there are various tactics to help ease your baby into this most unwelcome of tasks. A flannel cloth or sponge is perfect for cleaning your newborn baby's hair as this allows him to get used to the sensation of water on his head without the trauma of it splashing his face. Likewise a face shield placed on your baby's head will prevent water from splashing his face, and shampoo from stinging his eyes.

CRADLE CAP

A daily hair wash with a gentle, hypoallergenic shampoo helps to ward off cradle cap. Once cradle cap has set in, soften and remove the stubborn scales by rubbing olive oil onto your baby's scalp. Leave it on overnight, and gently remove the scales with a soft brush the next day. Leave cradle-cap scales that don't come off easily, as you could end up making your baby's scalp bleed.

Bathtime entertainment

Once your baby can sit up, bath time is another chance to play. Give your baby plenty of bathtime entertainment with plastic windup toys, bath books, and pouring cups, and watch him fill, pour, and splash water to his heart's content. If your baby is a reluctant bather, encourage him to associate water with fun by filling the washing-up bowl with water, splashing around together, and making bubbles.

Bathtime is also a great opportunity to bond with your baby. Talk to him, laugh together, and sing to make this a special time, or even have a bath together. Your older baby will love getting in the bath with you. Lay him on your chest, gently splash water over his body, and enjoy a lovely, long soak together.

AFTER-BATH CARE

Wrap your baby up in a baby towel with a hood after his bath to make him feel snug and safe, and then really indulge him with a relaxing massage. He will love the soothing sensation, and will feel warm, relaxed, and ready for sleep.

Skin care

Small babies are particularly prone to dry skin so treat your baby's skin with care and use only the gentlest of products. Bubbles in the bath can be fun, but they can also dry your baby's skin, so avoid bubbles if your baby has dry skin or eczema. Instead put baby oils or emollients in your baby's bath to prevent his skin from drying out and tackle dry patches by gently rubbing baby oil or olive oil into his skin.

Winter can be a drying time for your baby's skin. Put a bowl of water under his radiator when the heat is on to keep the air moist and give lots of fluids to keep him hydrated.

Eczema can make life miserable for your baby and for you. If your baby suffers with eczema, keep his fingernails short so that he doesn't break his skin when he scratches himself and put scratch mittens on him at night to stop him from damaging his skin, which makes it even itchier.

Clothes

Turn to pages 64–65 for advice on buying the right clothes for your baby.

Getting baby dressed

Changing your baby's soiled clothes can be an all-too-frequent activity. Don't despair if your baby hates being dressed and undressed—it's just a passing phase! Limit the stress by being gentle, smiling and talking him through each change so that this becomes a social time. Chatting to him in a singsong voice while you dress him will make him happier and more willing to go along with the task at hand. Play peekaboo with your baby while dressing him. Try cooing, "Where is baby?" while you quickly pass the top over his head—"There he is!."

Make your baby comfortable when you dress him by putting a soft towel on the changing mat, or by dressing him on the bed. Avoid stretchsuits that fasten at the back until your baby can sit up and don't pull your baby's arms and legs to get him into his clothes—pull the clothes to fit onto him! Your very young baby has a grasp reflex that can be put to good use when getting him dressed. Put the sleeve over his arm, and slide your hand up the other end of the sleeve. Then let him grasp your finger so that you can gently pull his arm through. Your older baby may love to wriggle and crawl off when you're trying to dress him. Join in the game! Pop his top over his head as he heads for the door, or tickle his tummy until he rolls onto his back and you can dress him with ease. As your baby grows, continue to keep dressing simple. A two-piece outfit is often easier to get on than an all-in-one if he refuses to keep still.

Hands and feet

Little bootees for newborns may look cute, but they can be more trouble than they're worth, as they often fall off and get lost. An all-in-one stretchsuit or some cotton socks will keep your baby's feet just as warm and snug. Skip dressing your baby in real shoes until he can walk, as they could damage the soft bones in his feet. Instead, soft leather bootees with elasticized ankles look great and leave his toes free to wriggle.

Whenever possible, leave your baby's feet bare in the warm indoors to help them develop and grow properly. Once your baby stands up and starts to cruise around, put him in socks that have nonslip soles so that you can both breathe more easily. As well as wriggling his toes, your baby's little fingers also love to fidget. As with socks, use mittens sparingly so that his hands are free to explore.

Hats

If your baby's skin is sensitive, protect his head from scratchy woolen caps by placing a thin cotton hat on his head, then putting the woolen cap over that. Your baby loses a lot of heat through his head, so put a hat on him when you're out together in the chilly winter. In the summer months, a wide-brimmed hat will protect his face and eyes from damaging UV rays.

Clothes for growing

Once your baby is mobile, he will need clothes that are more durable as well as comfortable. Buy larger sizes—but not so large that they hamper him—that don't restrict his movement and that he won't grow out of too quickly. Get the maximum wear out of trousers by buying ones that are too long and rolling the legs up. As your baby grows, just unroll the legs. Jeans are cute and really versatile, but be sure to choose those with soft denim to avoid rubbing and irritating your baby's tender skin.

Nighttime changes

Help your baby to learn to differentiate between day and night by changing his clothes before bedtime. Put pajamas on him or even just another sleepsuit, so that he starts to associate this time with going to sleep. When he wakes in the night, don't worry about changing his diaper unless he is noticeably wet or soiled. The less disturbance, the better the chance of him going quickly back to sleep.

Clothes care

Check labels before buying clothes and go for easy-care, washable fabrics. The endless stream of soiled baby clothes can make you feel chained to the washing machine so try soaking clothes overnight, and wait for a full load before turning on the machine. Wash bedding, wraps, and bibs at a high temperature to get rid of bacteria and dust mites. Opt for hypoallergenic baby detergents as these are gentlest on your baby's delicate skin and make sure that your baby's clothes are rinsed and dried thoroughly.

Teeth and teething

Your baby's first tooth is a moment of celebration for you, but it can be a real pain for him! If that first tooth pushing through is making your baby miserable, don't despair, there are plenty of tried and tested remedies.

Signs of teething

Excessive dribbling is a sure sign that your baby's first tooth is breaking through. Other signs include red cheeks, irritability, diaper rash, pain, ear pulling, refusal to eat, and night waking. Many mothers swear that teething is accompanied by fever, diarrhea, and a cough, and although there is plenty of anecdotal evidence to support this, check these symptoms with your doctor to rule out something more serious.

Teething remedies

Soothe your baby's discomfort with something hard and cold to chew on. A chilled, peeled carrot or teething ring can provide much needed relief. Also give him chilled water to drink. This has the double benefit of soothing his sore gums and replacing the fluid he has lost from dribbling. When he is irritable, apply pressure to his gums by gently but firmly rubbing your finger along them. This will bring relief and help to calm him down.

Homeopathic teething granules, available in health stores and many pharmacies, are also a popular remedy for sore gums. Ignore the old wives' tale that a touch of brandy on your baby's gums relieves soreness and gives him a good night's sleep! Never give your baby alcohol, even as a last resort.

Sometimes, a soothing cuddle can often be all the comfort your teething baby requires. When natural remedies do nothing for your teething baby, talk to your doctor about pain relief.

Cleaning teeth

Keeping your baby's teeth and gums clean and healthy is not only hygienic, but it also plays a role in the normal development of speech and appearance and good dental hygiene habits.

As soon as that first tooth appears, get cleaning. You can use a soft, damp cotton cloth to gently rub your baby's tooth and gums. Once your baby has two or more teeth, brush them twice daily with a baby toothbrush. (You can brush as soon as the first tooth appears, although a damp cloth will suffice for one tooth). A pea-sized amount of toothpaste is sufficient especially as it will be a while before he masters the art of spitting out. Use a toothpaste that is formulated for babies and young children. These have the correct amount of fluoride and do not have added ingredients, such as peppermint oil, which can irritate your baby's tummy.

Make teeth-brushing an enjoyable task for your baby. Turn it into a family event—your baby will love to watch you brush your teeth, and he will enjoy trying to imitate you. Bright-colored toothbrushes that feature favorite cartoon characters can also turn toothbrushing into a great game.

A diet for healthy teeth

A nutritious diet that contains plenty of calcium and vitamin C helps to build healthy teeth and gums in your baby whereas sugary foods and drinks cause cavities and gum disease. Avoid them altogether if possible, or limit their intake and brush your baby's teeth if he consumes them. Try to avoid juice drinks that contain teeth-rotting sugars. Instead, encourage your baby to develop a taste for water, and limit pure fruit juice, diluted with water, to mealtimes.

Crying

Crying is your baby's first means of communication. He is trying to tell you that he needs something, whether it is a clean diaper, food, extra blankets, or just a good old-fashioned cuddle. Your job is to figure out what it is he wants! Enlisting the help of an experienced mom—whether it's your own mom, a sister, aunt, or friend who has been there and done it— during the first week after the birth of your baby can be invaluable, giving you the confidence to cope on your own. Once you begin to understand why your baby is crying, it will be easier to deal with his cries and feel able to comfort him.

Why he's crying

As a new parent, you may find one of your main worries is whether you are able to work out why your baby is crying and so be able to soothe him. The key is to try not to panic and, often through a process of elimination, work through the reasons why he is upset. Soon you will be able to distinguish between a cry for hunger and a cry for a diaper change and meeting his needs will become second nature.

His basic needs

The most common reason that small babies cry is hunger. Don't try to hold out on your hungry baby by giving him a pacifier or finger to suck. A full tummy is all that will satisfy him. However, if he has been fed recently, check that there isn't some other reason for his tears before offering him food again right away, or he may expect to be fed each time he just needs a little comforting. A six-month-old who cries out in the night for food may be craving comfort more than a feeding. Try to hold off, reduce, and gradually phase out night feeding, so that you are eventually rewarded with an unbroken night's sleep.

Change your baby's diapers frequently to keep him comfortable, dry, and less likely to cry. Changes in temperature can be extremely upsetting for a newborn, such as the shock of cold air on his naked skin, so undress him in a warm room. If you need to get organized, say for his bath, wrap a towel around him to keep him warm and snug. On the other hand, excessive layers of clothes or blankets can make your baby hot and uncomfortable, so check to see whether his skin feels hot and clammy and remove layers if necessary.

YOUR BABY'S DELIVERY

Some babies who undergo a forceps delivery or a particularly long labor cry more than babies whose births were less stressful. Your newborn should settle down after a few days, but if you are worried, talk to your doctor.

All things in moderation

Overstimulation can be as distressing for young babies as understimulation is for older ones. Loud noises, cold hands, too-hot milk, bright lights, or too much bouncing or tickling all can prove too much and cause him to cry. Be sensitive to your baby's moods and alert to his energy levels. Games that delight him when he is wide awake can cause him to wail when he is tired or hungry and an overtired baby can be even harder to settle.

Separation anxiety

At about six months, your baby may experience "separation anxiety" and cry whenever you leave the room. Reassure him by explaining that you are going out and will be back in a moment—he will soon learn that you are not deserting him. Try not to be afraid to leave him with other people. Practice giving him to grandparents, other family members, or friends to hold while you calmly explain that you are going out of the room and will return shortly. On the other hand, if your baby screams when he is held by anyone else, be sensitive to his fears. Don't try to force him onto a person he finds upsetting, and reassure yourself that he will eventually grow out of this.

Returning to work can be a difficult time for everyone. If your baby screams whenever you leave him with his caregiver, try to reserve a few minutes to spend with him and the caregiver before you leave.

Waking himself

Twitchy sleepers can wake themselves with their jerky movements. If your baby regularly twitches and wakes, make sure that he is well wrapped in his blankets, or put him in a baby sleeping bag to prevent him from flailing about.

When he's unwell

Be aware of cries that may be the result of illness. If your baby has a fever, is off his food, or is inconsolable, it could be that there is something wrong, so check with your doctor. A cry of pain is easy to distinguish from other cries; if your baby lets out a shrill, urgent cry, go to him immediately.

Colic

If your baby has colic—a condition that is marked by persistent crying for two to three hours, often at the same time each day—don't beat yourself up thinking that you are somehow to blame. There are many causes and remedies given for colic. Milk that is given at the wrong temperature, too much or too little milk, gas, and a mother's diet have all been blamed. If nothing you try seems to resolve the situation, the best thing to do is probably to accept the crying and figure out how you will deal with a difficult few weeks.

If you do worry that there is something physically wrong with your colicky baby, check with your doctor, who will probably reassure you that it is just a part of your baby's development. Remember that he will grow out of this phase, usually at around three months.

Try to clear time each day for your baby's "colic hours." You will limit stress if you keep this time free from interruptions and tasks that can be done at other times. Take turns with your partner, if possible, during this time of day. For example, if your baby screams for two or more hours at a time, try doing half-hour shifts. Cradle your colicky baby tummy down along your forearm, with his head resting in your hand. This puts pressure on his abdomen and can help to soothe him. Lastly, try to give your colicky baby some quiet time each day, preferably in the early evening, when he is not overstimulated by a stream of visitors.

Comforting your baby

Some experts believe that by responding promptly to your baby's cries, you will increase his sense of security and make him better able to handle separation from you at a later date, so ignore any suggestion that going to your baby as soon as he cries will spoil him. Another popular myth is that of the "good baby/bad baby"— the "good" baby being the quiet, well-behaved one. Your baby cries because he needs something and ignoring his cries is not going to teach him a lesson. On the contrary, he is likely to be bewildered, cry even harder, and be more difficult to comfort when you do go to him. By seeing to him promptly, you will reassure him and increase his confidence, which should eventually reduce his crying.

Figuring out why your baby is crying will soon become second nature. At first, one cry can seem much like another, but as you get to know your baby, a little miracle happens and you begin to know exactly what it is that he needs.

Rocking and movement

Rock away your baby's tears. Babies love rhythmic movement, and some gentle rocking can often be just what your baby needs. Even better, walk around while you gently rock him—rocking combined with walking can work magic.

When all else seems to fail, put him in the stroller and walk around the block. You will be amazed at the speed with which his tears cease.

Close contact

Your baby may be crying out for the simplest of reasons—the need for contact, so holding him close and giving him a cuddle will give him the comfort he adores. There is evidence that babies who are regularly held close to their mothers cry less, so having plenty of contact will be mutually beneficial.

Hold your baby close and gently rub or pat his back. The double comfort of being held close and your soothing touch will soon wipe away his tears. A sling is a fantastic way to keep your baby close and get on with other tasks, such as household chores. He will love the closeness and constant movement, and probably forget all about crying.

Vary the position you hold your baby in to work out which works best for soothing him. Lay him tummy down on your arm, chest, or lap and gently rub his back, or hold him upright against your shoulder. Your baby will soon let you know which he prefers. Gently stroking his head can work wonders when you're trying to get him to sleep in his crib as he has contact with you, yet you don't have to pick him up.

Song and dance

Sing your baby a song. Don't worry about what or how well you sing—as long as it's vaguely tuneful, it's likely to have the desired effect. Alternatively, play your baby a tape of rhythmic, monotonous sounds, such as whale music, bird songs, or the sound of waves breaking. This "womb" music can be intensely comforting to him. If your baby is not too tired, put some music on and dance around the room with him. This is likely to prove such a great distraction that he will forget all about his tears.

Sucking

Small babies get great pleasure from sucking, so if your baby continues to cry, even after being fed and changed, offer him a finger—his own or your clean one—to suck away on. Or give your baby a sterilized, orthodontically approved pacifier to suck to give both of you some much-needed relief from constant crying.

Burping

Controlling your baby's gas can be the key to keeping him happy. Sit him upright and support his head to burp him. If you are bottle-feeding, check the flow of the nipple to make sure that he is neither sucking too hard nor gulping milk too quickly, both of which can make him swallow too much air.

Stimulation and frustration

Some babies are happy to sit and watch the world go by, but if your baby is constantly irritable, he may need more stimulation and get frustrated when he can't convey his needs. Take pre-emptive action to avoid frustration building. For example, don't leave him sitting in front of the same toys for an hour at a time if he hasn't yet learned how to crawl away. As his attention span is short, tears of boredom are never far away, so change his toys frequently to keep him happy and occupied. Similarly, keeping his toys well within his reach will stop tears brewing.

Distracting your baby is another form of stimulation and can help him forget about his tears. Point out plants, books, and lights, and show him the trees swaying outside the window. Before your older baby can move around on his own, he may get frustrated and upset when you leave the room and he is unable to follow. Don't just disappear—explain to him that you are going into the next room and will be back in a moment.

Routine

As your baby gets older, he will gain reassurance and comfort from daily routines. If he seems particularly unsettled by change, try to stick to a routine as much as possible, and introduce any changes gradually.

When your boy cries

Some experts believe that baby boys cry more than baby girls. Whether or not there is any truth to this, don't ignore your son's cries in the belief that this will toughen him up—it's likely to make him cry even more.

Keeping calm

The combination of extreme tiredness from broken nights and your baby's endless crying can test the endurance of even the most unflappable of parents. If it's all getting too much, do your best to stay calm and focused, and remind yourself that your baby is not going to cry forever. The more worked up you get, the more likely he is to sense your stress and may then cry even harder. If you do get to the point where you feel unable to cope, take steps before you get to breaking point.

TIME AND PATIENCE

Be patient. Give your baby time to respond to your chosen method of comforting. If you switch from one tactic to another, he will probably end up even more distressed than he was when you started.

Time out

If your baby's endless crying makes you feel like you're about to lose your cool, hand him over to your partner and take some time out. If you're on your own, put your baby down in his cot and spend a few moments in another room.

Having a break

If you find his crying draining and hard to cope with, try to arrange some time off while your partner does the babysitting and you recharge your batteries. Or let someone else—another family member or trusted friend—take over. Don't think that you are the only one who can comfort your baby. He may need a break from you, too, sometimes, and another pair of arms can be just what is needed to calm his nerves.

If you and your partner are shattered from sleepless nights, don't be afraid to ask for help from friends and family. Even a few hours' respite can refresh you and make you feel equipped to cope once more.

Talking to others

Try not to resent your baby's crying. It may seem that only your baby cries this much for this long, but that is almost certainly not the case. Talk to other moms about their babies and how they cope—you will probably be relieved to hear that your baby is actually pretty typical. Some parents like to give the impression that they have their baby's crying well under control, and that they never get flustered. Don't feel inadequate when this happens—just try to ignore their unhelpful bragging.

Goodnight, baby

There's no denying that the first few months of your baby's life can be exhausting and often trying. As small babies have shorter sleep cycles than adults, your baby goes from drowsiness to deep sleep and back to drowsiness in about 45 minutes, and is therefore likely to wake more often. However, once she starts on solid foods, she is likely to sleep for longer periods during the night. An agreed-upon strategy for sleep times and night waking is often what is needed to help you and your partner arrive at the other end of this sleep-deprived period with your sanity intact.

Where your baby sleeps

Don't feel the need to tiptoe around when your baby is asleep. Young babies usually find background noises, such as the washing machine or the radio reassuring, and they are likely to be lulled to sleep by them. In the early weeks, a transportable Moses basket lets you continue with what you are doing and keep an eye on her while she sleeps. Once she outgrows her Moses basket, a crib is ideal and will serve her well for the next couple of years. Turn to pages 68–69 for information about your baby's bedding.

Swaddling

Some experts recommend swaddling babies to give them a sense of security, while others think that freedom of movement is important. Take your lead from your baby—if she is happy being lightly wrapped up, there is no harm, but if she tries to kick free, don't struggle with trying to bundle her into a blanket.

Getting the temperature right

Check to see whether your baby is too hot or too cold by touching the skin on the back of her neck, and add or remove blankets as necessary. A room temperature of 65°F (18°C) is ideal for your baby's room. On chilly nights you can use a hot water bottle to warm the sheets, but never leave one in your baby's crib when she is in it, as it could scald her. Also beware of overcrowding your baby's crib with soft toys as too many could cause her to overheat, so stick to a few firm favorites.

SAFETY

Put your baby down to sleep in the "feet to foot" position to reduce the risk of sudden infant death syndrome (SIDS), also known as crib death. Lay her with her feet at the bottom of the crib so that she cannot wriggle down underneath the blankets and overheat or suffocate. Experts recommend putting newborns to sleep on their backs so they can breathe easily.

Your older baby may start to toss and turn at night and move onto her stomach to sleep. Being in that position is fine as long as she has developed the ability to move her head to the side to breathe easily.

Daytime sleep

During her first year, you and your baby are likely at some point to establish a daytime, as well as a nighttime routine. Whether this takes the form of daytime naps, most likely, or simply a quiet period during the day, it is often helpful to develop a routine, similar to the nighttime one, to help your baby to rest.

Winding down

A quiet period in the day helps your baby to wind down before her daytime nap. Read her a story, draw the curtains in her room, and put her in her crib with a favorite teddy. Some babies are happy to sit and play in their cribs during the day without going to sleep. If your baby prefers to do this, don't force her to sleep—some quiet time off her feet will suffice as a rest.

Getting her to sleep

Some babies love to fall asleep in a sling, warm and close to your body. This is also because your baby is comforted by gentle movement—after all, she has just spent nine months swaying around in your womb. Gentle rocking, whether in a sling or in your arms, is often enough to send her into a deep slumber.

If your baby refuses to sleep during the day, but is irritable by the end of the afternoon, it could be that she just doesn't want to miss out on any fun. Take her for a drive in the car or a walk in the stroller to get her to sleep, and to ensure that she gets the rest she needs for her growth and development. Some believe that restless babies are said to have more active brains, so if your baby seems to wake at the slightest noise, take comfort in the thought that she may be bright, inquisitive, and social.

When she won't sleep

It's fine if your baby still needs two naps a day as she approaches her first birthday, as long as she is sleeping well at night. On the other hand, don't battle with her to get her to sleep during the day when clearly she doesn't want to—you will just frustrate yourself and her. Take the lead from your baby. If she starts to refuse one of her daytime naps when other babies you know still regularly nap during the day, accept that is the way she is. It's pointless to try to force her to sleep when she doesn't want or need to. Be positive when daytime naps get dropped. You may find that this actually frees up your time, allowing you to get out and about more with your baby rather than being tied to the house whenever she needs to sleep.

Nighttime sleep

In the first few weeks, your baby won't be able to distinguish between night and day. As long as she is not hungry, wet, too hot, or too cold, she will sleep soundly no matter where she is. After this period, you can help her to distinguish between day and night by opening the curtains and stimulating her when she wakes in the day, and quietly soothing her in a darkened room when she wakes at night. Once she starts to tell the difference you can think about setting a bedtime for her.

Giving her lots of stimulation each day with new sights and sounds and plenty of fresh air will keep her busy and will help her to sleep soundly at night, although beware of overstimulating her before bedtime. Above all else, be patient when trying to get her to sleep at night. She is unlikely to fall asleep right away, so sing her a lullaby, gently rock her, and stroke her head to lull her into the land of nod.

Putting her down

Some advance planning can help to make the transition from your arms into the cot a smooth one. Lower the sides of the crib or raise the mattress so that if she falls asleep in your arms, you can put her down without the risk of waking her as you set her into her bed. Feeding her close to her cot will mean you don't have far to go to put her down when she falls asleep. Likewise, preparing your baby's bed before you put her down will mean that you don't have to rummage around, getting blankets ready and removing toys, and so increasing the chance of her waking. An obvious, but often overlooked, tip is to cradle your baby in whichever arm you will use to put her down—you don't want to have to maneuver her into your other arm once she is asleep in order to lay her in her crib. Once you have successfully put her down, stroke her head so that she isn't startled awake by the sudden loss of contact with you.

Try to put your older baby down while she is still awake so that she masters the art of going to sleep on her own. If she uses a pacifier, aim to wean her off this after two to three months, or you may find yourself getting up at night simply to replace it. A soothing tune from a windup musical mobile attached to her crib can be the perfect lullaby to help her drift off.

Creating a nighttime routine

As your baby grows, she needs to learn to go to sleep on her own. Earlier solutions, such as rocking and pacifiers, will delay this transition and make bedtime harder for you both. Wean her off these, and create a relaxing bedtime routine instead. Try a warm bath, a story, and an evening breast- or bottle-feeding to calm your baby and help send her off into a blissful sleep. Some soothing classical music before bedtime can be just the thing to relax your baby and get her in the mood for sleep. Or sing her a lullaby yourself—this can work wonders in helping your baby to nod off, and she really won't mind if you're out of tune. Make a little ritual out of saying goodnight to your baby's favorite teddies. Once you have kissed them, point out that they are all fast asleep—with luck, she will follow suit.

Keep bath time for older babies for the end of the day. They need a bath to wash off all that food and grime, and a warm evening bath helps your baby to relax, wind down, and feel ready for sleep.

Don't feel that you can't leave your baby's room until she is tucked up under the blankets. Your older baby may even refuse to sit down in her crib. Say good night, pat her on the head, and leave. If she cries out, wait a few moments, then repeat the routine again. She will eventually settle down. A comfort object such as a teddy, a soft toy, or a favorite blanket acts as a replacement for you, giving your baby a feeling of security and helping her to drop off into a peaceful sleep. If she regularly settles down on top of her blankets, wait until she is fast asleep before you go in and rearrange her.

Night waking

In the early weeks be prepared for the night shift. Young babies need plenty of sleep, but this is unlikely to fit in with your sleep pattern. Go with the flow and adapt to your baby's sleeping times rather than expecting her to fit in with you.

Getting her back to sleep

Make a minimum of fuss when your baby wakes at night. Don't stimulate her with chatting—feed and change her quickly, then put her back down. She will soon learn that nighttime is not playtime. Cloth diapers are less absorbent than disposables, so you might consider using a disposable at night, even if you use cloth diapers during the day. If she simply stirs, she may not need feeding or changing: try to soothe her by stroking her hair, singing to her, and talking to her in a quiet, hypnotic voice and resist the temptation to lift her out of her crib, so that she doesn't come to expect to be taken out and cuddled. Above all else, avoid using the stroller or car as a sleep aide at night, or you may find yourself on regular midnight jaunts.

Make sure that you and your partner have the same techniques for getting your baby back to sleep. If one of you always strokes her head and the other always lifts her up and rocks her, your baby will get confused, and she'll be unlikely to respond well to either method.

When she is hungry

If your baby begins to wake at night when previously she'd been sleeping through, this may be a sign that she needs more food during the day. Increase her milk intake, or, if you think she is ready for weaning, supplement her milk with baby rice.

Breast-fed babies may continue waking in the night longer than bottle-fed ones, because they may more closely associate comfort with food. Give your baby a large feeding before bedtime, waking her if she falls asleep before she has finished. Your partner may have more success settling your breast-fed baby when she wakes at night, as the moment she sees and smells you she will expect more than just a cuddle.

After a couple of months, try to hold off feeding your baby as soon as she wakes in the night. Comfort and soothe her, then, if necessary, feed her. She will gradually go longer between feeds. Dilute milk or formula with water at night, slowly increasing the amount each night, so that your baby learns it's not worth her while to wake in the night for food. By the time she is six months old you can discourage nighttime feedings altogether by offering her water when she wakes rather than the breast or formula.

NIGHT LIGHTS

A night light in your baby's room can stop you stumbling and waking the whole household when you check her at night. On the other hand, a night light isn't essential, and introducing one to your baby's room could lead her to think that the dark is something to be afraid of. If you would rather your baby did not become reliant on a night light, you could install a dimmer switch so that you can see your way around in the dark without waking your baby.

Sleeping together

Putting your baby down to sleep in your own bed may be appealing, but she is more likely to wake in the night, especially if she is breast-fed and can smell food close by. Talk to your partner about sleeping arrangements. In the first few weeks, having your baby in bed may seem ideal, but you could find that your relationship with your partner suffers if this becomes a long-term arrangement.

Leaving her to cry

The older your baby gets, the more prolonged a bedtime battle can become. If you can bear it, leaving her to cry it out can sometimes break the whole crying-checking cycle. You can either leave her to cry for a long period if you can bear it, or leave her for a couple of minutes when she wakes at night to see if she goes back to sleep on her own. If she continues to cry, go in and try to soothe her. Gradually extend the time before you return, and repeat this over a period of nights. Soon she should begin to feel more secure and fall asleep on her own, happy in the knowledge that you are never far away.

Letting your baby cry it out when she wakes in the night can be as difficult for you as it is for her. Don't worry that you are psychologically damaging your baby by leaving her to cry at night. Some experts think that this is the best way for your baby to learn to fall asleep on her own. But if you find leaving her just too difficult then don't try it, as you will just end up even more stressed. Always check on your baby if she sounds truly distressed. Her foot could be stuck between the crib bars, or she may be unable to free herself from her blankets.

Teething

At about seven months, your baby may wake at night with teething pain. Often, a quick cuddle will settle her. If she has a fever, talk to your doctor before giving her any medicine.

Getting yourself to sleep

If you find it hard to fall back to sleep when your baby does at night, try a relaxation technique so that you at least get some rest time while your baby sleeps. A baby monitor may help you to relax at night, knowing that you will be able to hear your baby cry, even from down the hallway.

Early waking

The occasional five or six o'clock start to the day is more or less manageable, but when this becomes a daily occurrence, fatigue levels can soon escalate to the point where you're not sure for how much longer you can function on a rational level. Rather than resign yourself to bedtime at nine o'clock each night in order to cope with your baby's early mornings, consider some strategies that may allow you to reverse the trend.

Encouraging her to wake later

If your baby is up with the larks each morning, you may be putting her down too soon in the evening; try delaying her bedtime a little more each night until she wakes at a more bearable time. As well as monitoring the time she goes down at night, keep an eye on her daytime naps. By around six months, your baby needs less daytime sleep. If she wakes with the dawn, you may be letting her sleep too long during the day.

If your baby wakes early even after you have altered her sleep time, don't jump out of bed each morning as soon as she stirs—she may fall back to sleep or be happy to amuse herself for half an hour while you enjoy some valuable rest time. Likewise, if your early riser is greeted with a cup of milk or breakfast each morning as soon as she's up, you may be encouraging her to continue waking before you are ready to start the day. Soft toys in your baby's crib or attached to the bars, or a colorful mobile over your baby's crib may keep her occupied and amused when she wakes, and she might be less likely to call for you straight away. On a practical note, putting up dark curtains with a thick lining in your baby's room can often do the trick and put an end to those horribly early mornings.

Some babies just naturally wake early, and there's nothing to do but to start the day when your baby does. If this is the case, you may simply have to resign yourself, and go to bed earlier to cope with the early mornings. Taking it in turns with your partner to do the early morning shift can help to lighten the load.

Sleeping through

This will happen eventually, although you may not believe it. In the meantime, there are some practical steps you can take to hurry this magical day (or night!) along. You can help your baby sleep through the night by ensuring that she gets plenty of calories during the day and reducing the time she stays on the breast at night. Moving your baby into her own room can often be the key to her sleeping through the night as she is less likely to be disturbed by your movements or snoring, and you are less likely to jump up the moment she whimpers. Don't be tempted to cut out your baby's daytime sleep before she is ready in an effort to get her to sleep through the night as, if she is exhausted by the end of the day, she is more likely to have a fitful night's sleep.

Getting out and about

It's easy to get cabin fever in those first couple of weeks, so take the plunge and get out with your baby. You'll find your first trip together an exciting and liberating experience. Don't be overly ambitious on your first outings together. Stay a short distance from home—a nearby park, perhaps a friend's for coffee—and gradually build up to longer trips when you feel more confident. As well as giving you and your baby a change of scenery, a new baby provides you with a great opportunity to meet new people and try new activities. Find out about local mother-and-baby groups, baby music groups, or baby massage classes.

Baby transport
Turn to pages 74–76 for information on baby buggies, strollers, and car seats.

Car travel
You may anticipate that driving with a small baby will be a fraught and stressful experience, but this doesn't have to be the case. As long as you are prepared and time your journey well, driving with your baby can be an enjoyable and peaceful time.

Car entertainment
Small babies usually fall asleep on long car journeys, but your older baby may need to be entertained. A tape or CD of children's songs and a soft toy or a book will keep her occupied. Be prepared for long car journeys with your older baby by taking along some nutritious snacks and water in a lidded cup.

STAYING CALM

Fill up with gasoline when there are other adults in the car, if possible, so that you avoid the stress of trying to fill the car and placate your screaming baby at the same time. When you're driving, never let yourself be distracted by your baby in the car for even one moment. If you find your baby's screams impossible to ignore, take a pit stop. Pull over at the next convenient place or, if you're on the highway, take the next exit, rather than stopping on the shoulder of the road. Calm your baby, feed and change her if necessary, and give her a toy to distract her, then set off again.

When to travel

Try to time your car journeys to ensure they are peaceful and stress-free. For instance, set off when your baby is tired and due for a nap rather than after her sleep, when she is more likely to be restless. Your older baby may be too excited to sleep on journeys so setting off after her nap time will mean that she is alert and interested rather than tired and grouchy.

Time long car journeys for around your baby's bedtime. Feed, wash, and change her, then let her begin her night's sleep in the car. You will probably find that you barely disturb her slumber as you transfer her into a crib when you eventually arrive at your destination.

Being prepared

Leaving the house with a baby can take a lot longer than you anticipate. Although dirty diapers and hungry babies are often beyond your control, thinking about what you need in advance and having a bag ready to go will make exiting the front door, and your subsequent trip, a whole lot easier.

Your baby's bag

Have a changing bag ready so that you can head out of the house quickly without feeling like you are planning a major expedition. Keep the bag stocked with baby wipes, diapers, diaper bags, cotton balls, bibs, and any other essential items. Choose a changing bag that has several compartments (at least one of which is waterproof), a travel changing mat, and an insulated pocket for bottles.

Even if you usually use cloth diapers, you may prefer to take disposable ones on outings with your baby and always take a couple more than you think you'll need. Baby wipes are worth their weight in gold when you're out. As well as making diaper changing a breeze, they are great for cleaning yours and your baby's hands, mopping up spilled milk, and cleaning baby food off clothes and furniture.

If you can't get to a baby changing room when you're out, improvise by changing your baby in the back seat of the car, in a quiet spot in a park, or even in the car trunk. Most large department stores have baby changing facilities, and some have an area where you can feed your baby in privacy.

For long trips, be equipped with a first-aid kit. This should contain adhesive bandages, gauze pads and strips, antibacterial cream, scissors, and a thermometer.

Clothes

Take a spare set of clothes—or two—for your baby when visiting friends or going on outings and take additional clothes if you are going to be out for any length of time with your baby so that you can add layers if the weather cools.

Toys

Take along some toys for your baby when visiting friends and family. A few amusements will keep your baby happy for an hour or two and make the visit a pleasant, rather than a stressful, experience. Be as economical as possible when packing toys for a trip. Opt for a familiar favorite, such as a car, stuffed animal, or musical toy, as well as a couple of books and perhaps a new toy (for the novelty factor).

All-weather protection

Your baby's skin is extremely delicate and she is unable to regulate her body temperature as efficiently as you, so it's important to dress her appropriately and protect her from hot and cold weather.

When it's cold

Your baby cannot regulate her body temperature as efficiently as you, and she loses a lot of heat through her head, so keep her warm when you are out in the cold weather with a wooly hat. When it's really freezing, a hat with ear flaps does the job. In the winter months, keep her cozy in her stroller with a leg-and-toe cover that zips up like a sleeping bag and wrap her well with a hat, mittens, and a cozy blanket. Before taking her out in the cold feed her, as the body uses up more calories to keep warm.

Protect your baby from the elements with a pull-down hood attached to her stroller and attach a rain cover to prevent your baby from getting drenched in a downpour and to protect her sensitive skin from cold, biting winds. Never stay out with your baby if her clothes get wet unless you have a spare set to change her into.

When it's warm

Overdressing your baby in warm weather can cause her to overheat, and it may bring on a prickly heat rash, so dress her in lightweight, loose-fitting cotton clothes that protect her from the sun's rays but don't leave her sweating. As well as clothes, use a parasol to keep the sun's rays off her and schedule outings on hot days for early morning and late afternoon to keep her out of the sun when it is at its strongest and most damaging.

Your baby can't tell you when she is thirsty, so ward off dehydration when it's hot by offering her frequent drinks. Never be tempted to leave your baby in a parked car in hot weather while you pop into a store, as the temperature in a stationary car can quickly soar to dangerous levels.

Sun protection

Until your baby is more than six months old, avoid using sun protection creams on her without first checking with your doctor. Instead, keep her covered with sensible clothing to protect her from sunburn and dehydration. A wide-brimmed hat that shades her eyes and neck gives good protection. You may want to choose one with a flap at the back that covers the whole of her neck, for extra protection. Never sit out your baby in direct sunlight and if you are walking her in the stroller, attach a parasol or sun canopy to it to keep her shaded.

After six months protect your baby with sunscreen and clothing even when she is in the shade. Her skin is sensitive, and it should be protected with a minimum SPF of 20. If she is fair-skinned, use a total sun block and when choosing a sun protection cream, look for one that protects against both UVA and UVB rays.

Your older baby may wriggle and resist when you try to apply sunscreen, so don't wait until you are out in the sun—apply the cream indoors about half an hour before you plan to go out, and then reapply your baby's sunscreen if she has been in a pool or under a sprinkler. Make sunscreen an essential diaper-bag item and, very importantly, don't forget about your own sun protection! It's easy to be so busy protecting your baby from the sun that you neglect yourself, which sets a bad example to your baby and puts you at risk.

Swimming with your baby

Once your baby has had his immunizations, at about four months, check out the local pool. Many community centers have parent-and-baby classes run by accredited teachers and enjoying the water together will be relaxing for you and stimulating for your baby. Baby pools are smaller and warmer than adult pools, and your baby is more likely to relax in them and enjoy the water. Don't take your baby into a swimming pool or other body of water until her head control is good enough that she can keep her head lifted above water. This could be as late as four or five months. If your baby really objects to being in the water, then don't force her into a pool. Although it's a good idea to get her used to water, before the age of three she is unlikely to learn how to swim, so take a break and try her again in a few weeks', or even a few months', time. It's a good idea not to make your baby reliant on floats, water wings, or swim rings to keep her afloat in the water. Instead she should be supported and supervised by an adult at all times.

If you are not relaxed in the water, get someone else who enjoys swimming to take your baby into a pool, or she may pick up on your anxiety and develop a fear of the water herself.

Feeding away from home

Feeding your baby when you're out is easy. She isn't fussy about where she gets her food—a park bench is as good as a café, and is probably less stressful. You can breast-feed or bottle-feed, or take food in a lidded container with a spoon, a bib, and something to wipe up the mess. If you're using formula, ready-to-use cartons are perfect for days out. These require no refrigeration—simply take along a sterilized bottle, and when you're ready to feed him, open the carton and pour the formula into the bottle. Store-bought jars of prepared baby food are quick and convenient for outings. Just take along a plastic bowl and a spoon, or even feed her straight from the jar. Be ready to clean up any mess quickly by packing plastic bags for dirty clothes, cups, spoons, and bibs. For days out with your older baby take a selection of nutritious snacks along. Raisins, bread sticks, and fruit will ward off hunger between meals and prevent you from resorting to sugary snacks.

For a special treat, take yourself and your baby out to lunch at a restaurant. Most restaurants provide high chairs, and many are happy to heat up brought-along baby food or formula.

Supermarket shopping

Grocery shopping with a small baby needn't be a chore. Try putting your baby in a sling and leave your hands free to push the cart around, select food, and load the car without having to transfer her from car seat to cart seat and back again. Also take advantage of any baby-friendly facilities, such as parent and child parking spaces, carts that have a baby seat, and wider checkout aisles. On shopping trips with your older baby, take along a snack and something for her to drink to keep her busy.

Staying away from home

Going on vacation, or even having a short stay over, can seem like a logistical nightmare. As with many aspects of parenting, being prepared and advance planning make all the difference. Do beware of introducing changes to your baby's routine when you are away, such as weaning from breast to bottle, as vacations inevitably cause disruption anyway and so are not the best time to make changes that could be better left for your return home.

What to take

Sterilizing tablets for your baby's bottles, rather than an actual sterilizer, and extra thin absorbent diapers, take up the minimum of space and so are perfect for traveling. A fold-away travel crib is a worthwhile investment—it takes up little space, and it allows you to set up a crib for your baby wherever you go. Avoid unnecessary luggage. If you are renting a car, check if the rental company provides baby car seats on request. If you love to hike, invest in a baby back carrier once your baby can hold her head up unsupported. Lightweight and easy to pack, these are perfect for vacations and everyday use.

Flying and going abroad

Traveling abroad with your baby is easy as long as you are organized. Make sure her immunizations are up-to-date, and check with your doctor if you think she may need additional vaccinations for your destination. Your baby cannot travel on your passport, so get a passport for her well before you take a trip abroad. If your child is on medication, take a spare prescription in case her medicine gets spilled or lost while you're away.

Book airline seats in advance if you are flying with your baby. Some airlines have sky cribs for babies, and a front-of-section seat enables you to make use of this. If you can afford to, book an extra seat so that you can all enjoy some space and move around more easily.

Breast- or bottle-feed your baby during takeoff and landing to prevent her from getting a painful earache. You can take bottles of formula onto a flight, which the flight attendants should be happy to heat up for you. For your older baby, take additional water and snacks to keep her hydrated and happy during long check-ins and possible delays. Sometimes snacks for the flight are a good idea, as the food served on airplanes is often high in sodium; it is worth checking the airline's meal options before the flight, however, as some companies, especially long-haul ones, provide baby food or alternate snacks that can be ordered in advance.

If you are traveling to a new time zone, try to re-establish your baby's eating and bedtime routines as soon as possible.

Hotels and vacation homes

Cut down on your luggage by checking before you leave whether
your hotel provides travel cribs. Likewise, many vacation homes
are well equipped for babies and children, with high chairs, crib,
videos, and games, so find out exactly what's available so that
you can avoid unnecessary packing. Some baby-friendly hotels
not only supply cribs, but also offer a babysitting service so that
you and your partner can enjoy a relaxed meal while someone
else watches your baby.

Beware that not all family-friendly hotels are baby friendly.
Check the hotel's facilities before you book your room as some
hotels cater to older children, with clubs and adventure play
areas, but have little to offer in the way of facilities for you and
your baby. Avoid altogether hotels which don't state that children
and babies are welcome. A stay in such a place is likely to prove
stressful, and you may feel slightly unwelcome.

Where to go

Be realistic about the sort of vacation you plan. Gone are the
days when you could spend two weeks touring art galleries.
Instead, parks, zoos, and landscaped gardens are all easier than
art galleries or enclosed spaces where you will be struggling to
keep your baby quiet and well behaved. So try to arrange for a
leisurely pace without too many planned trips that could cause
more stress than they're worth.

Caring for your sick baby

It's all to easy to panic when your baby is unwell, but bear in mind that most illnesses are minor, and that they actually assist in the development of your baby's immune system. Being listless, off his food, feverish, vomiting, or having diarrhea are all clear indications that your baby is unwell, but should not cause undue concern. However, if any of these is severe or prolonged, don't hesitate to speak to your doctor. Above all else, trust your instincts. You know your baby better than anyone, and if you think that he is not quite right—even if you can't put your finger on what exactly is wrong—don't be afraid to talk to your doctor. Give your sick baby plenty of tender, loving care. A kiss, a cuddle, and some soothing words will go a long way toward reassuring him and putting him on the road to recovery.

Fever

You can usually spot a fever in your baby by his flushed cheeks and hot forehead. Before you decide to give him medicine, take his temperature to confirm your suspicions. Liquid crystal strips, which are placed on the forehead to determine a baby's temperature, are inexpensive and easy to use, but are not particularly accurate. A digital thermometer, which is held under the armpit, is more accurate, but it can be tricky to use on a fidgety baby. Ear thermometers are easy to use and accurate, but considerably more expensive. Don't take your baby's temperature orally—thermometers should not be placed in children's mouths until they are at least seven years old.

You can reduce fever and the misery it causes by offering your baby plenty of drinks, by not overheating him with blankets and clothes, and by giving him medicine, such as acetaminophen or ibuprofen, to lower his temperature. When all other measures fail to reduce your baby's fever, sponge him with lukewarm water. Undress your baby and cover him with a light blanket. Expose one part of his body at a time, gently wiping it with a sponge soaked in tepid water. Dry him thoroughly and dress him. Ignore any advice to "starve a fever." Your baby needs more calories, not less, when he is ill, however, don't fret if he refuses food—he will soon regain his appetite.

GIVING MEDICINE

Try to relax your baby before giving him medicine, and always give the recommended dose at the right intervals. If your baby is particularly fretful when you give him medicine, try using a dropper. Support his head on your arm, and hold his arm to stop him from trying to push the dropper away.

Feeding your ill baby

Continue to breast-feed your baby if he has a tummy ache, but check with your doctor before giving him formula or anything else that is not breast milk. For your older baby, keep the fluids flowing. He is likely to lose his appetite when he's unwell, so it's doubly important that he gets plenty to drink to prevent him from dehydrating. Don't be tempted to offer your older baby sugary snacks if he is off his regular food. Bananas, milk, and raisins all go down well, and they give him the vitamins and minerals he needs to fight off his illness. If you are weaning your baby, you may find that the introduction of a new food brings on a bout of diarrhea. If you suspect that a certain food is to blame, withdraw it and try it again in a couple of weeks.

Don't put pressure on your baby to eat when he's unwell, as this could create a feeding problem in itself. Although you may be alarmed that he hasn't eaten properly for days, try not to worry—he is sure to make up for lost time when he recovers. Babies don't starve themselves!

Nighttime comfort

Ease nighttime congestion by raising your baby's mattress slightly at one end. This will help prevent his nose from getting stuffy so that he gets a better night's sleep.

When to get help

Call the doctor if your baby has an unusual rash, excessive vomiting or diarrhea, vomiting or diarrhea that lasts for more than 24 hours, or a temperature above 38°C (100°F). Call, too, if he has difficulty breathing or is inconsolable. It's normal for your baby to be drowsy and to sleep a lot when he's unwell, but you should always be able to rouse him. If you can't, make sure you call the doctor immediately.

FIRST AID

Learn some rudimentary first aid. In the unlikely event of your baby losing consciousness, you will probably be the first person on the scene, so some basic knowledge could prove invaluable. Make sure that your baby's caregiver has some first-aid knowledge and knows what to do in an emergency.

Immunizations

Keep up-to-date on your baby's immunizations. His first, which are given at around eight weeks, protect him from polio, diphtheria, tetanus, whooping cough, and some types of meningitis. If a fever coincides with an immunization date, talk to your doctor about postponing the appointment until your baby is better. A mild fever is common after an immunization, so it's worth having some acetaminophen or ibuprofen on hand to give to your baby if necessary after an injection.

There are small risks attached to any vaccine. When you're weighing the pros and cons of immunizing your baby, however, remember that many serious illnesses have been virtually eradicated today thanks to immunization.

Feeding

Breast-feeding

Everyone is familiar with the mantra "breast is best" and official guidelines back this by recommending that you give your baby nothing but breast milk for the first six months. Although breast-feeding should be the most natural thing in the world, it can prove surprisingly hard for some mothers and babies, so don't feel like a failure if you need advice or reassurance. Make good use of the hospital's breast-feeding counselor for helpful hints and tips, as the better your—and your baby's—technique, the smoother and more enjoyable an experience breast-feeding will be for both of you. Whether it's a breeze or an uphill struggle, once you have a smooth feeding routine underway you will find that breast-feeding is the perfect way for you and your baby to bond.

Feeding after the birth

Colostrum is the fluid that you produce during the first few days of breast-feeding, and it gives your baby valuable protein, minerals, and antibodies. If you are separated from your baby after the birth, talk to the hospital breast-feeding counselor about expressing milk until your baby is well enough to breast-feed.

Breast-feeding benefits

As well as containing exactly the right amount of nutrients and water that your baby needs, breast-feeding provides your baby with a whole range of benefits. The antibodies in your milk protect her against common infections during her first few months, and there is evidence that breast milk can protect against eczema and other allergies. What's more, as breast-feeding works by supply and demand, it's difficult to overfeed your baby as your body will produce exactly enough milk for her needs. There is rarely a need to supplement her supply of breast milk with formula. When she needs more milk, her sucking will prompt your body to produce more!

Keeping up your strength

You need around 2,500 calories a day when you're breast-feeding to keep your energy levels up and ensure that you have a good milk supply for your baby, so it's important that you eat a nutritious, balanced diet and drink plenty of fluids. Make sure that you have regular meals with healthy snacks between meals, and keep a drink of water on hand while breast-feeding to replenish the fluids your body loses in breast milk.

FOODS TO AVOID WHEN BREAST-FEEDING

Avoid eating peanuts while breast-feeding, as this may trigger an allergy in your baby, particularly if there is already a family history of allergies. If your breast-fed baby has excessive gas, it may be the result of something you are eating; cut out foods such as cabbage, brussels sprouts, beans, and citrus foods and drinks to see if this makes a difference.

How your baby feeds

At birth, your baby's stomach is about the size of a walnut, and she can only drink a little milk at a time, which is why she feeds little and often. As she—and her stomach—grows, she can take in more milk and go longer between feedings. Hence the first few weeks of your baby's life can seem like a nonstop feeding marathon, but take comfort in the thought that, when she's about two months old, your baby will go longer between feeds and you can start to establish a feeding routine. Once your baby can go for two to three hours at a time without feeding, outings are far less stressful, so you can get out and about together.

You can help your baby to feed by providing her with a calm environment. Feeding time is not the time to stimulate your baby—she needs to concentrate on the task at hand, so don't be tempted to distract her with toys.

Newborn babies just love to suck, so if she still seems hungry after a big "meal," try giving her a pacifier. Alternatively, she may be going through a growth spurt. These occur at around three weeks, six weeks, and three months, so if your baby suddenly seems to need more milk, there may be a good reason.

Mixing breast-feeding and bottle-feeding in the early weeks can cause "nipple confusion" for your baby. If you want to give her a bottle as well as the breast, try to limit this to one bottle a day.

Getting comfortable

A breast-feeding session can last up to 40 minutes or more, so gather everything you need, such as a drink, a book, the remote control, or the telephone, before settling down to feed your baby. Your baby will latch onto your nipple more easily if you get as comfortable as possible before you start. Try lying on your side or using cushions for support to help you relax and enjoy each feed. A high-backed chair with cushions to support your arms is also comfortable and helps you to concentrate on positioning your baby. Breast-feeding after a cesarean section can be tricky so use soft pillows or cushions to raise your baby to breast height so that you don't lean forward and put pressure on the wound. Nursing pillows are a good investment. The L-shaped pillow sits around your waist, giving your baby firm support while keeping your arms free to have a drink, read a book, or make that phone call! These pillows are also great for breast-feeding twins, as you can lay one along each arm of the pillow.

As well as feeling comfortable and relaxed, a good nursing bra is essential. The cups unhook or unzip, making it easy to get your baby to your breast without getting into a fluster. Breast pads inside your bra between feedings will absorb any leaked milk and avoid embarrassing stains.

Sore nipples

Sore nipples make breast-feeding stressful for you and your baby. To help prevent discomfort, make sure that your baby is latching on properly to the whole nipple and its surrounding area. Never pull your baby off your breast, as this can be painful! Instead, gently insert a clean finger into her mouth, then release your nipple. If you're really struggling, get practical guidance and advice from a breast-feeding counselor.

You can also prevent nipples becoming tender by rubbing some breast milk onto them after each feeding as the antibacterial properties in your milk will help prevent your nipples from getting sore. Other popular remedies for sore nipples include chilled cabbage leaves or damp flannels, which can be wonderfully soothing placed on sore, swollen breasts, and exposing your nipples to the air whenever possible will help to keep them clean and dry. Nipple shields help you carry on feeding if your nipple is sore and cracked as they give your nipple a chance to heal while allowing your baby to continue feeding.

Your milk supply

The size of your breasts is irrelevant when it comes to feeding your baby. Small-breasted women are just as able to produce enough milk, and they should ignore any suggestion to the contrary. Breast-feeding little and often in the first couple of weeks will stimulate your breasts to produce milk and build up a good supply. Gently massaging your breasts when breast-feeding encourages the milk flow and helps prevent your breasts from becoming engorged, or too full. It's common for a breast-fed baby to gain weight more erratically at first than a bottle-fed one but, as long as she is thriving, it is unlikely that she is being starved!

Breast-feeding can be exhausting, so catch a nap whenever possible to allow your body to refuel. This is not indulgent—your body needs plenty of rest to ensure that it produces an adequate supply of milk for your baby. If you are concerned that you're not producing enough milk, keep breast-feeding! The more you put your baby to the breast, the more milk your breasts will produce. Within a day or two, you will meet the demands of your hungry baby. However, if your baby really won't settle down after a large feed, check for other signs of discontent before giving her more milk. Burp her, check her diaper, and gently rock her to see if these help to soothe her.

Make sure your baby empties one breast before moving onto the next so that she doesn't miss out on the calorie-rich hindmilk that comes at the end of the feed. If you're not sure if your baby has emptied a breast, gently squeeze your nipple to see if any milk comes out.

If your newborn baby sleeps for long periods during the day, it is worth waking her for a feeding so that your breasts are stimulated to continue to produce milk. If she regularly falls asleep when she's feeding, gently stroke her cheek to stimulate her sucking reflex and help her finish her meal.

POSSETTING

Burping your baby after each feeding will help to stop her bringing up milk, known as possetting. Sit her on your lap or lay her, tummy down, over your lap and gently rub her back. Once she can support her head, hold her over your shoulder and gently rub or pat her back. Try not to despair if your baby seems to regurgitate most of her milk. This is very common, and the amount brought up usually looks greater than it actually is. If, however, she is vomiting violently, or it really does seem like an excessive amount, talk to your doctor.

Expressing

There are plenty of reasons to express milk: you can enjoy an evening out while your baby gets the benefits of your milk; your partner can get involved in feeding; you can catch up on a few hours of sleep by getting your partner to do the last feed of the evening; and you will boost your milk supply. An extra supply is also handy when your baby has a growth spurt, and once your baby starts on solid foods, you can mix expressed milk with baby rice. Expressed breast milk can be refrigerated for 24 hours and frozen for up to one month so invest in a manual or electric breast pump and get expressing!

Stopping breast-feeding

Deciding when to stop breast-feeding can be a hard decision to make, but try not to fret that your relationship with your baby will suffer once you stop. You may find that it actually improves as you spend less time feeding and more time socializing together. If you're returning to work during your baby's first year, make sure she will accept the bottle well in advance of your return date so that you are not left worrying about how she will be fed when you're not there. On the other hand, returning to work doesn't mean that you have to stop breast-feeding altogether. You can continue your early morning and late night feeds for as long as you wish. Avoid weaning from breast to bottle altogether when there are major changes going on in your baby's life, such as the family moving to a new house.

When you decide to stop breast-feeding, wind down gradually: stopping suddenly may cause your breasts to clog up with milk. When you are weaning your baby from the breast to the bottle, replace one feeding each week so that your breasts slow down their milk production gradually and your baby isn't moved abruptly from the breast. Start with the feeding time that she is least interested in, such as the mid-afternoon feed. The first breast-feeding in the morning and the last one at night are about comfort as well as food, so they are often the last to be dropped.

If she refuses to move from the breast to the bottle, try giving her bottled expressed breast milk. She may be happier to try the already familiar taste from another source, although, as she recognizes you by your smell, she may be reluctant to take a bottle from you when she knows that what she likes best—your breast—is so close by. If this is the case, get your partner to try giving her a bottle—he may have more success.

Bottle-feeding

Although breast milk is the ideal food for babies, formula contains all the nutrients necessary for your growing baby and is tailored to meet the changing needs of your baby's digestive system at different ages. Bottle-feeding also has the added advantage of allowing Dad to become more involved. The key to successful bottle-feeding is organization. From preparing batches of feeds in advance to keeping bottles scrupulously clean, a well-rehearsed routine will transform what can be a hard grind into a simple everyday task.

Getting equipped

You will need around eight 8-oz bottles and a couple of 4-oz bottles; about eight to 10 nipples (extras are necessary, as these can easily split); a sterilizer; formula and a scoop; and a bottle brush for cleaning. Medium-sized nipples are usually best, as they prevent your baby from drinking milk too quickly or too slowly. Take the cue from your baby: if she gulps down an 8 oz bottle of formula, you may need to change the nipple to one with a smaller hole so that she can drink her milk at a more leisurely pace. Nipples that split or become worn should be discarded.

Preparing bottles

Take the hard grind out of bottle-feeding by preparing all of the day's bottles in one batch and storing them in the fridge. Measure out formula to the exact quantity recommended on the packet, using a knife to level off the scoop, and being careful not to pack the formula in. If you make up bottles of formula incorrectly, your baby could gain weight too quickly.

Babies usually prefer milk that is slightly warm rather than cold so warm up filled bottles by standing them, unopened, in a bowl of hot water for several minutes. Check the temperature of the bottle by shaking it, then dripping a few drops of the warmed formula onto the inside of your wrist. The milk should feel lukewarm—neither too hot nor too cold. You can gauge how much to bottle-feed your baby by her weight. She should have around $2^1/_2$ oz (70 ml) of milk for each pound of her body weight.

Transporting bottles

There's no need to feel housebound when you're bottle-feeding your baby as it's easy to transport bottles and formula milk. Picnic bottle bags, which are specially insulated to keep your baby's bottle cool, are great when you're out with your baby and most eating establishments are more than happy to heat up a bottle. Prepackaged, ready-to-drink cartons of formula are also ideal for days out. Bring along a sterilized bottle, and just pour the formula into it when you're ready to feed your baby.

Cleaning bottles

It's important in the first year to sterilize all bottle-feeding equipment to prevent bacteria from building up and making your baby ill. Before sterilizing, all the bottles and nipples should be thoroughly washed with a bottle brush in warm, soapy water. Never save any milk or formula that's left over in the bottle, even if your baby has only managed to drink a little from the bottle and don't leave bottles lying around unwashed. Rinse the formula or milk out right away—even if you leave the sterilizing until later—as bacteria can build up quickly. Steam sterilizers, specially designed for baby bottles, are the easiest way to sterilize.

Supplementing bottle feeds

Formula does not contain the thirst-quenching foremilk of breast milk, so if you are bottle-feeding, your baby is more likely to be thirsty, especially in hot weather. Give her some cooled boiled water to supplement the formula and quench her thirst.

PREVENTING GAS

Bottle-fed babies are more likely to suffer from gas, so make sure that you hold the bottle at such an angle that the milk covers the whole nipple to prevent your baby from swallowing any air.

Cups

Moving to drinking her milk from a cup is a big step for your baby, but the earlier you introduce one, the more likely she is to drink from it. If she refuses to take milk from a bottle, you could try moving straight to a cup. However, don't force a cup onto your baby. If she refuses to drink from it, leave it for a week or two before trying it again.

Experiment with different types of cups until you find one that suits your baby. Cups with two handles offer her a secure hold, although some babies prefer no handles—they simply grip the cup. Cups with tops and spouts control the amount of liquid she gets and prevent her from gagging. Help her by holding the cup with her and encourage her to take a few small sips at a time. If she insists on holding the cup herself, allow her to assert her independence.

First foods

Milk starts to play a less prominent role in your baby's diet once he increases his intake of solids, although, until he is a year old, it will still form the basis of his diet; starting him on solids during this time is more a matter of getting him used to new flavors and textures. However, although his main source of nutrition still comes from milk, the process of learning to eat forms a crucial part of your baby's social development, as he is learning the invaluable art of eating and communicating with others, which will stand him in good stead throughout his life.

Weaning

Current advice suggests waiting until your baby is six months old before weaning him. However, if you're exhausted from breast-feeding, your baby doesn't seem satisfied, or you're returning to work, you may consider weaning early (see below).

Early weaning

Until he is at least four months old, your baby finds it hard to digest anything other than milk and weaning him too early carries the risk of giving him a food intolerance or allergy. However, if your baby is large and has a healthy appetite, talk to your doctor or health-care provider about weaning him earlier than is normally recommended. He or she may suggest supplementing his diet with baby rice. Most importantly, follow your own instincts: don't let other people's opinions make you feel that you should start your baby on solids before you think he is really ready for them.

Ready for weaning

Look for the signs that your baby is ready for more than just milk. If he is no longer satisfied after an 8-oz bottle or a full breast-feeding, the period between feedings is shorter, and he is waking again in the night, he is probably ready for solids.

Baby rice

Baby rice is the perfect first food—it's bland, gentle on your baby's stomach, and enriched with vitamins and iron. Your baby is unlikely to reject it, and it will get him used to eating something besides milk. Choose a time when your baby is not too hungry to give him his first sampling of baby rice. Breast- or bottle-feeding him first can take the edge off his hunger so that he will be more receptive to the new experience. Mix baby rice with breast milk, formula, or cooled boiled water until it is a smooth consistency and give your baby just a small mouthful at a time from a plastic weaning spoon. Don't skimp on your baby's milk feedings once you've started him on baby rice, as at this stage milk is still his most important food and source of vitamins and minerals.

How to feed your baby

The easiest way to feed your baby his first solids is to sit him in a free-standing baby seat. These seats enable you to sit him semi-upright, strap him in securely, and keep your hands free to spoon food into his mouth.

Give your baby time to adapt to eating with a spoon. Until now, his sucking reflex has been his only means of getting food, and he may try to continue with this method. Put a small amount of food on the spoon so that he doesn't sputter. He will gradually learn to get the food to the back of his mouth and swallow it.

Moving to a high chair

Once your baby can sit up easily, it's time to transfer him to a high chair. Choose one that is secure and easy to clean, with shoulder and crotch straps to keep him safely locked in, and look for a high chair that is padded, comfortable, and sturdy enough to take the weight of your baby. Make sure that the chair is placed on a level, nonslip surface. Seats that screw on should only be used on sturdy, well-supported tables—never attach one to a glass table or to any table that has an unattached tabletop. If your baby is swamped by his high chair, put cushions or rolled-up towels in it to prevent him from slipping around.

Expanding your baby's menu

Once your baby has mastered the art of taking baby rice from a spoon, you can start to introduce new tastes and textures to his diet, but beware of turning mealtimes into a battleground. You may have eagerly anticipated starting your baby on solids, but it's a new, and not necessarily welcome, experience for him. If he screws up his face and spits out each new offering, stay calm and try again. If necessary, give up with good grace and try the food again at a later date.

Trying new foods

Introduce new foods one at a time. Start with a single vegetable or fruit puree for a few days, then try a new flavor. This way, you can keep track of any digestive upsets, withdraw the food that's responsible, and wait a couple of weeks before trying it again. Be guided by your baby's taste buds. If he rejects a food outright, don't force it on him or offer no alternative. Instead, give him something else, and try the rejected food a week or so later.

Once your baby is used to eating certain foods, you can make life more interesting by combining foods to create new flavors. By introducing as wide a range of foods and flavors as possible, you can help to prevent your baby from becoming a fussy eater later on.

Your baby's mealtimes

Build up your baby's mealtimes gradually, starting with just one solid meal a day to begin with. Increase this to two meals in the second month and three in the third month. Stay close to your baby's side at mealtimes and don't be tempted to leave the room even for one moment, as he could quickly choke on his food.

Once you start him on solids, be prepared for some mess! Your baby is likely to transfer more food into his hair and onto the floor than into his mouth, but try to take this in your stride and limit the chaos by putting newspaper on the floor, a bib on your baby, and rolling up his sleeves.

Fruits and vegetables

Fruit and vegetable purees are good follow-ups to baby rice. You can keep the consistency smooth by cooking the fruits and vegetables until they're soft, pureeing, and, if necessary, straining them. Like adults, babies are known to have a sweet tooth, so start your baby on vegetable purees before he has a chance to develop a preference for the sweeter fruit ones. If your baby finds little appeal in a bowl of pureed green beans, try sweeter vegetables, such as carrots, sweet potatoes, and peas. Once you start to combine foods, you can make life sweeter by adding fruit purees to the less desirable vegetable ones.

Wash, peel, and core fruits before you cook and puree them and, until your baby is about five months old, avoid giving him fruits that contain small seeds, such as kiwis, strawberries, or raspberries. If you do introduce these early on, strain them through a sieve to get rid of the seeds. If you're out and about, mashed ripe bananas are the convenience food of choice for babies. No heating, pureeing, or freezing is needed—just a fork for mashing!

You don't need to turn cooking for your baby into a daily chore. Instead, cook fruit and vegetables in batches and freeze them in ice cube trays or clean yogurt containers, then defrost one or two cubes for each meal.

Keep it natural

Go organic. If you're worried about introducing pesticides to your baby, it may be worth paying a bit extra for organic fruit and vegetables. Or if this is beyond your price range, get rid of any harmful pesticides on fruits and vegetables by peeling them whenever possible and washing them thoroughly before your baby eats them.

New textures and tastes

As your baby gets used to eating solids, you can start to vary the consistency of his food; even before his first tooth appears, he can practice chewing with his gums, so don't feel that everything you give him needs to be pureed.

Adding firmness

Mash, rather than puree, his meals so that he has to work that little bit harder. Mashed ripe pears, peaches, plums, and apples should all be big hits. Grate fresh fruit and vegetables to add to your baby's repertoire of textures and gradually reduce the cooking time for vegetables to make them slightly firmer, steaming them to preserve the vitamins and minerals. Once your older baby can manage lumpier textures, you can give him the same food that you eat, as long as it contains no added sugar or salt and it is not too fibrous. Simply prepare the meal then, before you add seasoning, set aside a portion for your baby.

Variety and flavor

Make sure that your older baby is offered a wide variety of foods, and try to avoid falling into the trap of offering him his favorite foods too often: he could miss out on a variety of minerals and vitamins, and become fussy about trying other foods.

At about nine months, start to add herbs and garlic to your baby's diet. The sooner he tries new tastes, the less likely he is to reject them. Toward the end of your baby's first year, give him small pieces of pasta with freshly cooked sauces. It's easy to prepare, and the variety of shapes and colors will appeal to him.

Iron intake

It's important to include iron in your baby's diet after six months, when the supply he was born with runs out. Follow-on milk contains iron, and you can introduce fortified baby cereals, vegetables, legumes, and meat to his diet, too. Liver is a fantastic source of iron for your older baby. It's easy for him to chew and digest, and, even if you don't like the taste, he may love it.

Introducing protein

Between six and nine months you can start to add protein to your baby's diet. Although this is a great source of iron for your baby, after the mild flavors of his fruit and vegetable purees, he may find the taste too strong so serve meat with fruit purees or a milk sauce to make it more palatable and choose high-quality meat, avoiding processed meats, such as hot dogs and lunchmeats. At this stage, make sure meat is finely chopped, by hand or in the food processor, or buy freshly minced meat from your butcher. Make sure you remove the skin from chicken, and any fat and bones from meats.

Eggs are a good source of protein, but introduce them gradually. Avoid hard-boiled eggs before six months, and soft-boiled eggs until your baby's first birthday. Flaky white fish is also an excellent source of protein, but be thorough when checking for bones. Buy fillets of fish and go through them carefully after cooking them to remove any stray bones.

WHAT TO AVOID
The key to giving your baby the best nutritional start in life is to keep things as natural as possible. Fresh, home-cooked ingredients that include plenty of fruit and vegetables will provide your baby with the optimum diet for growing and glowing! But there are some things that a small baby just can't stomach, so it's worth reminding yourself of the pitfalls (see opposite).

Allergy alert

You can add cow's milk to your baby's food at six months, but don't give it as a drink until his first birthday and avoid it altogether for the first year if you have a history of allergies or lactose intolerance in the family. Again, if allergies run in your family, avoid giving eggs to your baby before he is one year old. The same applies to foods containing gluten, such as wheat, barley, and rye, and fish.

Hazardous foods

Never be tempted to add salt to your baby's food. His kidneys cannot digest too much salt, and you may be creating a habit that could lead to high blood pressure later on. Honey may seem like a healthy food for your baby, but it's not safe until he is a year old as it can contain a bacteria that, although harmless to adults, could cause botulism, a serious condition, in your baby. Nuts and shellfish are strictly off limits until your baby is two years old and whole nuts should be avoided until he is five because of the risk of choking. Steer clear of foods that your baby could easily choke on, such as whole grapes or olives—chop these until your baby is thoroughly adept at chewing.

Hidden ingredients

Check cereals for their sugar and salt content. Many cereals claim to be nutritious and they may contain an impressive list of vitamins, but quite a few are also loaded with sugar and salt, neither of which are any good for your baby.

Your baby's tableware

Before the introduction of solid food your baby was used to
simply sucking when he was hungry. Now comes the challenge
of learning how to eat from a bowl and drink from a cup!

The first tea set

At first it will be you who spoons the food into your baby's
mouth. However, before long he will start to show an interest in
feeding himself. As soon as he shows a desire to hold a spoon,
let him, as the more freedom he has to experiment, the sooner he
will succeed. Have another spoon handy to feed him yourself so
that some of the food makes it into his mouth.

Drinks and drinking vessels

Your baby may develop more of a thirst once you start him on
solids, so give him some cooled boiled water or diluted baby fruit
juice with his meals. A cup of diluted, unsweetened fruit juice
will help his body absorb the iron in the food he eats, but try not
to let him fill up on juice before his meal, leaving him with little
appetite for his actual food. If he refuses drinks (other than milk)
from a bottle, try giving him a trainer beaker. A cup with two
handles may be easier for him to hold, or you can give him a
helping hand by holding a handle to help him guide it to his
mouth so that he takes small sips and is less likely to cough.

EATING OUT

Eating out at a restaurant with your baby may seem daunting,
but it can be perfectly manageable. Choose a child-friendly
establishment, and bring a couple of toys to keep him occupied.

Food safety

In both the preparation and storage of food, be sure to follow the guidelines on good kitchen practice.

Cleanliness and hygiene

Be super-hygienic in the kitchen. Wash your hands before and after preparing food, especially if you have been touching raw meat, and wash them again before feeding your baby. Be scrupulously clean about the area where your baby eats. Wash the surface thoroughly after each meal, as your baby will be very happy to pick at and eat any dried-up food that's stuck to the table, and choose a plastic bib that is easy to wipe clean. Once food has made contact with your baby's bowl, spoon, or fingers, don't be tempted to save it for the next meal.

Storing food

Be vigilant when storing and saving food. If you are doubtful about a food's freshness, throw it away. Don't keep foods past their expiration date, and discard the remaining contents of opened jars within the recommended time. Cool cooked foods quickly and store them in the fridge or freezer and store other perishable foods in the fridge. When using jars of baby food, remove the amount you need for one meal, then store the jar in the fridge. If your baby wants more than one serving, use a clean spoon to take more food from the jar before returning it to the fridge. Transfer food from a jar into a bowl before giving it to your baby. If you do serve it straight from the jar, throw away any food left in the jar after that meal. When freezing foods for your baby, make a note of the date you freeze it, and use it or throw it away within the recommended time.

Finger foods

At about nine months, your baby may want to assert his independence after months of being passively fed. This is a great time to get him started on finger foods, such as toast, raw or gently cooked vegetables, pieces of fruit, and slices of cheese. As well as being ideal snacking fodder, finger foods make a wholesome meal, and will broaden your baby's taste horizons. Moreover a cold, peeled stick of carrot or celery or a slice of toast are great for him to gnaw on when he is teething.

Add to the attraction

Make finger foods tempting and attractive by preparing foods in different colors and shapes, or jazz up finger foods by serving them alongside a fruit or vegetable puree for your baby to dip into. Miniature sandwiches are easy to prepare, and your baby will love them. Experiment with different fillings such as cottage cheese, mashed bananas, and grated cheese and apple.

FINGER FOOD HAZARDS

Cut finger foods into large pieces so that your baby can bite off what he needs, rather than giving him small pieces that he could put into his mouth whole and choke on. Dried fruits may seem like great finger foods, but don't give your baby too many, as they can have a laxative effect!

Snacking

To turn snacking into a healthy pastime, skip the sweets and give your baby breadsticks, fruit, cheese, rice cakes, and raw vegetables such as bell peppers, carrots, and celery between meals. Healthy snacking can ensure that your baby gets his daily nutritional needs. Time snacks so that they won't interfere with main meals, and don't give snacks for the wrong reasons—if your baby is bored, distract him with a toy rather than with food, or he could learn to view food as a consolation and have weight problems later on. Sit your baby down for snacks as well as for meals. Letting him walk around with food in his mouth is not only unsafe and unhygienic, but it will also do nothing for his table manners!

Eating together

Eating alone is not much fun, especially for your sociable baby, so make mealtimes social events and sit down and eat together whenever possible. Your baby will discover that mealtime can be fun, and he will also learn from watching you eat. If you can't eat at the same time as your baby, sit down and talk to him when he is eating so that he doesn't think of mealtime as a lonely time.

How much should your baby eat?

Be guided by your baby's appetite. Put small quantities of food on your baby's plate as large portions can be off-putting and then give him a second helping if he's still hungry. If it's a battle to get your baby to eat more than a couple of mouthfuls, make his food more appealing by cutting it into interesting shapes, or by putting different-colored foods on his plate.

Your baby may prefer to eat little and often. If sticking to three meals a day is too restricting, give him nutritious snacks between meals. You may find that your older baby is irritable by dinnertime and finds it hard to concentrate on his food, in which case it might be a good idea to make lunch the main meal of his day and turn dinner into a more relaxed affair.

Playtime

Playtime

Your baby is programmed to play, and for good reason. Play is vital to your baby's development. Through play, she learns about herself and the world around her, and picks up the skills she needs to thrive in that world. Learning how to play helps your baby develop her social skills, stimulates her senses and increases her ability to observe, concentrate, and develop her manual skills. Furthermore, evidence suggests that babies who are not given the chance to play can have difficulty learning later on, so give your baby a head start in the world by encouraging her to play.

The wonder of you

You are your baby's first playmate and she learns more from you than from any toy. Simply by loving her, talking to her, and involving her in everything you do, you will be teaching her far more than you could imagine. Apart from helping her to learn, time spent playing with your baby is also time spent bonding.

Your baby loves to explore your face with her eyes, and later with her fingers, and she listens for your voice. Talking and singing to her will entertain her and help her with her language development. So make eye contact, talk to her, and use exaggerated facial expressions to stimulate and delight her.

Listening to your baby

Your baby is unique, so take your cue from her. If she is quiet and sensitive, rough-and-tumble play may overwhelm her. On the other hand, she may be endlessly curious and in need of plenty of stimulation.

Your baby's changing moods

Be aware of your baby's moods and try to tailor her play accordingly. If she is feeling lively and happy, she will enjoy energetic play, such as being tickled, but the same activity could upset her when she is tired or cranky. Constant stimulus is too much for any baby. When she is tired or hungry, it's pointless to try to get her to play until her basic needs have been met.

Encouraging your baby

You may be eager for your baby to master new skills, but it's best to accept that she will do things only when she is ready. The best way to help your baby learn is to encourage and praise her when she attempts something new. If she senses that you are anxious for her to learn new skills, she may start to believe that she can never please you, so take things slowly and give her plenty of time to react to objects and events. What comes easily to you will take her a lot longer, so try to go at your baby's pace and give her a chance to figure out how to respond to things. Show her that you think she is wonderful by praising her with hugs, claps, and exclamations of "aren't you clever!" whenever she masters a new skill.

Standing back and letting your baby take the initiative can be difficult, but try to resist the urge to take over. Instead, be led by your baby. For example, if she shows an interest in the red ball, don't try to divert her attention to another toy. She will be pleased if you show an interest in her choice, and you will boost her self-esteem. Encourage your baby's individuality. If she plays with a toy in an unusual way, don't try to correct her. Let her experiment on her own, as long as she is safe, to help her develop her creativity.

Toys and stimulus

Toys and playtime are not optional extras for your baby, they are actually an incredibly important part of her development. Toys are your baby's learning tools—helping to stimulate her during each stage of her development. Don't feel though that you need to break the bank providing your baby with every possible toy: with a little thought and imagination, you can create play items from the simplest of objects. Also, many areas have a local toy library, which, for a small fee, allows you to replace your baby's toys on a regular basis.

Early stimuli

In the first few months, the majority of your baby's stimuli comes from simple sources, such as bright lights, finger play, and tickles, all of which will entertain and intrigue her. Babies also like bold patterns. In her first six weeks, she will probably show more interest in simple black and white designs. You can make your own pictures for her with a thick felt-tip pen and then hang the pictures in her crib to give her visual stimulation.

In the first few months, your baby responds to toys that make a gentle noise, such as a rattle or a squeaky animal, and she enjoys toys with faces that she can study, such as teddies and dolls. A baby gym provides plenty of opportunities for play as she grows and develops. When she can do little but lie on her back, she will be entranced watching the bright toys moving. Once she can wave her arms around, she will enjoy hitting the toys and making them swing to and fro.

Crib toys

A simple mobile hung above your baby's crib is an ideal first toy. It not only gives her something to watch, but it also helps her learn about movement. Once she starts to move her arms around, she will love to swipe at toys that make a noise when she touches them, such as a rattle. She will also enjoy looking at soft toys tied to her crib, which later she can reach out and touch.

Keep it simple

Your baby's concentration span is limited, so give her just a few toys at a time that she can give her full attention to rather than overwhelming her with dozens of different toys. Think, too, about how you present her toys. If they are scattered all over the floor, this is stressful for you and confusing for your baby. The more inviting her toys look, the more she will be encouraged to investigate them, so lay them out side by side rather than dumping them in a pile.

Simple toys can sometimes be the best. Your older baby may gain as much, if not more, pleasure from pots, pans, and a wooden spoon as from her regular toys. Older babies also love to empty and fill containers. A cardboard box with some toys in it that she can take out, put back in, and take out again, will no doubt delight her. Likewise, your baby will get hours of fun from plastic bath beakers that she can fill up with water and empty.

Building blocks or cardboard boxes are another firm favorite. Help your baby to build them up, then watch her have fun knocking them down again. Be inventive with household items. An empty paper-towel roll makes a great telescope for your baby. She can also indulge her love of putting things to her mouth by using it as a loudspeaker.

If you use your imagination, you will encourage her to do the same. For example, sheets of paper may not seem like a great play item to you, but your baby will get heaps of fun from crumpling, tearing, and crackling them. And an old phone with the wires removed will not only give your baby endless fun but also, as she babbles away, she will develop her language skills. Plastic lidded containers filled with rice or dried beans, which your baby can shake, will also get the thumbs up—she'll be intrigued by the noises and learn about cause and effect.

Your baby's changing needs

Your baby changes constantly throughout her first year and so therefore do her needs. Toys for younger babies may fail to hold her attention, while an older baby's toy could be too complex and possibly dangerous, with small parts she could choke on.

Once your baby sits up and starts to move around, give her toys that have switches, buttons, and dials, such as activity centers, that she can manipulate and which will help her to learn about cause and effect. Don't be tempted to give your baby toys that are too old for her in an attempt to speed her development. She will progress when she is ready and trying to push her too quickly could set up a pattern of failure and frustration.

Storing toys

Baskets, trunks, and plastic boxes are all ideal for storing toys. Or otherwise, designate a floor-level kitchen cupboard for your baby's playthings. She can spend hours emptying and filling it, and it will distract her from other cupboards that you don't want her to meddle with. Turn keeping toys orderly into a fun game by making a den for your baby under the kitchen table. Put toys under the table and pop your head under with a cry of "peekaboo."

Playing and learning

As your baby grows, she rapidly acquires new skills, the majority of which are picked up through play. Play allows your baby to learn and develop and so increases her confidence and self-esteem. Make learning fun; games that help her to pick up new skills in a relaxed setting offer the best learning environment.

REPETITION

Your baby repeats actions over and again to reinforce what she has learned. If she wants to play "drop the toy and you pick up" ten times in a row, try not to get impatient—instead, spend some time helping her to perfect her new skill.

The world of make believe

Toward the end of your baby's first year, he will start to use his imagination more. A strainer, saucepan, or rolling pin will be just as exciting to him as his actual toys. Encourage this experimental play by engaging him in role-play. For example, give him a paper towel so that he can imitate you as he "helps you" clean the house.

One to one

Before your baby learns to play with toys, he will love spending time exploring you! Being held close to you, smelling you, exploring your face with his fingers, and enjoying a cuddle together is heavenly for you and reassuring and comforting for him.

It's impossible to spend all day playing with your baby, but do try to set aside some one-to-one time each day to sit and play together. Simple activities will delight and amuse your baby, such as gently bouncing him up and down on your lap. He will probably respond with glee, and the activity will help him to learn how to socialize with you. Or get down to your baby's level. By sitting on the floor with him and helping him with his toys, you will be encouraging his muscle and hand-eye co-ordination.

TIME ALONE

Give your baby some playtime alone. While one-to-one play is immensely important to her, independent playtime helps her to develop her imagination—so, during her "alone" time, keep an eye on her, but keep your distance.

Your baby's growing awareness

At about six months your baby learns about cause and effect. Give him a soft ball that he can roll away and toys that he can pull along. Help your older baby experiment more when he plays by giving him objects that he can empty and fill, such as plastic containers and empty cereal cartons.

At about seven months, your baby understands that objects exist even when he cannot see them. This increased awareness adds to his sense of security, as he knows that his toys and games—and you—are always there. By his first birthday, your baby is quite inquisitive, and he loves to experiment with different shapes. Give him toys that fit into one another, such as a set of nesting bowls, shape-sorters, or just different-sized cartons.

Exploring through touch

Once your baby can reach out and touch, she will enjoy exploring different textures. Give her objects and toys to feel, and talk to her about whether they are smooth, furry, rough, hard, or soft. A "feely bag" is a great way for your baby to explore textures. Fill it with baby-safe items of different textures and shapes. These don't have to be toys—they can easily be pieces of material, paper, or balls. Some toys incorporate different textures, such as a play mat or a touch-and-feel book, which encourage your baby to explore the world through her fingers.

When she is about three months old, she may start to pick up and hold objects. Put a selection of different-textured objects in front of her—for example, a leather bag, some silky pajamas, a wooden spoon, and a wooly top—and let her touch and explore each item. As she practices picking up toys she will also discover that some things are heavier than others.

Games to play

Boost your baby's confidence and awareness by playing simple hide-and-seek games. The classic game of peekaboo never fails to delight. Cover your face with your hands and say, "Where's mommy?" Then uncover your face and happily exclaim, "Peekaboo!" Or put a baby blanket over your head and ask, "Where's mommy? Have you seen mommy?" Then whisk the blanket away and exclaim, "Here she is!" This will never fail to amuse your baby. On the same theme, let her see you place a toy under a cushion, then encourage her to uncover the toy.

Play laughing games with your baby. Whether you make funny faces or do a silly dance, she will be sure to find you highly amusing, and you can both enjoy laughing together. Or play listening games to help your baby take notice of the world around her. When an airplane flies over, or a siren screeches past, ask her if she heard the noise, and tell her what it was.

New concepts

As with hide and seek, your baby has not yet grasped the concept that when something is out of sight it still exists. Give your older baby a container with a lid that she can place objects in. By opening the lid and seeing that the objects are still there, she learns that things still exist even when she can't see them. Or play "choo-choo trains:" "drive" a toy train behind a chair, and say "choo-choo" as it emerges at the other end. She will soon expect the train to re-emerge at the other end, and she'll be ready and waiting for it.

On the move

Your baby is constantly expanding her repertoire of movements. From learning to pick up objects to sitting upright in a chair to starting to crawl, she is broadening her horizons all the time. Encourage her at each stage of her development by providing her with toys that suit her abilities and enhance what she has already learned.

Give your baby plenty of playtime on the floor so that she has ample opportunity to use her arms and legs and develop her mobility skills. Or change her perspective by giving her some time on her tummy, some on her back, and some propped up and secured in a chair or with cushions on the floor.

Soon enough your baby will be making her first attempts to crawl and will be eager to explore the world around her. Make her playtime safe by putting covers on plug sockets, moving breakable items, and supervising her closely while she explores.

Once she is on the move, give her toys that she can move along with her, such as cars, balls, or pull-along toys. Make crawling into an adventure! Buy a play tunnel for your baby to crawl in and out of, or make a homemade tunnel by taping together some open-ended cardboard boxes.

Before your baby is able to walk, put her in a baby bouncer to show her how exciting the world is when you're on two legs. Strap her securely into the baby bouncer, attach it to a door frame, then watch her spring up and down. Once she has progressed to standing, make learning to walk fun with a push-along walker. Some double up as activity centers so that your baby has plenty to entertain her.

Never pressurize your baby into physical games or activities that she is not ready for. For example, if she screams when you put her on the baby swing, take her out and sit her on your lap while you gently swing on the big swing.

Hand-eye co-ordination

Help develop your baby's hand-eye co-ordination by giving her a soft ball that she can pick up, roll, throw, and drop; or introduce her to shape-sorting toys, which she'll love as she gets older.

Using her hands

Once your baby masters the art of picking something up, give her a rattle with two handles as this is easier for her to grip, and will help her develop her manual skills as she learns to pass it from one hand to the other. Encourage your older baby to develop her manual skills by giving her some toilet-paper rolls with which to build a tower and which she can then knock back down!

Reaching out is a difficult skill for your baby to learn. Encourage her to reach for an object by waving a rattle near her hands. Once she has reached for it, shake it while it's in her hand so that she knows she has grasped it. Once your baby can sit unsupported, roll a soft ball to her to encourage her to bring her hands together to catch it. Activity boards, building blocks, and even soft dolls and teddies all encourage your baby to find new ways to use her fingers, and they help her develop essential skills that she'll use later on, such as self-feeding, holding a pen, and brushing her teeth.

Action games

At two to three months, you can start to play gentle physical games with your baby. Bend her knees, stretch out her arms, and talk to her in a singsong voice about what she is doing. When she is lying on the floor, encourage her to turn her head by getting down to her level. Lie on the floor next to her and hold up a toy for her to look at.

Once your baby is about three or four months old, you can take hold of her hands and gently pull her up into a sitting position. Make this into a game by singing a song or nursery rhyme as you pull her up. You can also help your baby strengthen her leg muscles with weight-bearing games. Stand her on your lap and encourage her to take the weight on her legs. Be a climbing frame for your baby: once she is mobile, lie down next to her and let her climb up and over you. Or be your baby's playpen: sit on the floor and circle your legs around her, then fill the circle with lots of toys.

Before she can speak, your baby will communicate through signs, such as a wave of her hand to signal bye-bye—let her know that you understand what she is referring to.

Stimulating the senses

Choose toys that stimulate your baby's senses, such as animals that squeak, brightly colored rattles, and a teddy with a bell attached. Your baby will enjoy toys that make noise, but select ones that make a gentle, musical sound rather than loud, squeaky toys that could damage her hearing. Stimulate your newborn baby by attaching bright toys to her stroller. These will help her develop her visual skills while she looks at the different shapes and colors. Babies are also fascinated by faces so go through the family photo album together and talk to your baby about all the different people in it.

Color

Play color games with your baby. Concentrate on one color at a time and point out several objects in that color. By focusing on one color, she is more likely to absorb the information.

BOOKS FOR BABIES

Babies love books, and it's never too soon to introduce your child to them. Once she is a few months old, your baby will enjoy some quiet "playtime" sitting on your lap and looking at a simple board book. Show her picture books that feature animals, and make each animal's noise as you point to its picture. She will soon start to recognize the animals and become familiar with the sounds they make. Your baby will enjoy the interaction with you, and you will be helping her to develop her intellectual skills.

Types of play

Whether you're indoors or outdoors, in the depths of winter or sweltering in the summer heat, there is never a shortage of activities and play ideas for you and your baby. Playtime doesn't need to be a complicated affair and sometimes it's easy to turn the most mundane events into fun and games.

Water baby

In the summer months, treat your older baby to water play. Fill a bowl with water and give her some plastic cups and spoons to splash about with. Get outside and blow bubbles for her to watch and burst, or fill a bowl with water and a bit of dish soap, whisk up the water to make bubbles, and watch her play with them.

Add fun and variety to bath time with floating boats, spongy squeeze toys, and magical water wheels. Equally good are made-up bath toys. Be inventive with a strainer to pour water through, a sponge to squeeze, and a plastic jug to pour with; all will give your baby as much enjoyment as any store-bought toy. Even better, have a bath together. Teach your baby how to splash her hand in the water while she lies along your tummy.

Structured play

Try to add structure to your baby's day to prevent her from getting frustrated or bored. Alternate her toys to give her new stimuli and take her on regular outings to the local park or around the neighborhood to let her see what is going on outside. As well as activity and stimulation, give your baby some quiet playtime each day with one-to-one attention from you. Read her a story, show her some pictures, or sing some nursery rhymes.

Playing with others

Encourage your baby's social skills by inviting other mothers and babies to play and socialize with you. At this age, your baby will simply play alongside other babies (this is known as "parallel play"), but this is an important first step in learning to get along with others. As your baby's first birthday approaches, take her to a playgroup. Even playgroups that are primarily for toddlers usually have a "baby" play area, and you will have the opportunity to meet other moms there.

Imaginative play

Once your baby can hold her head up, play flying games. Lie on your back with your legs in the air and lay your baby along the length of your shins, with her head facing yours. Glide your legs slowly backward and forward as she laughs with delight. Your baby also loves to be rocked and swayed. Pretend that she is an airplane by holding her face-down in your arms and flying her in a circle.

Everyday games

Turn dressing, undressing, and diaper-changing into fun and games by tickling your baby and gently blowing on her skin. Other everyday events can also be transformed into playtime. When your older baby holds up her arms to be picked up, swoop her up with a cry of "wee!" and swing her around in a circle.

Outdoor play

You don't have to save the kiddie pool for hot weather. Fill it up with water and put leaves, toy boats and cups in it for your baby to splash around with. Once your baby can walk, put some waterproof boots on her and take her out to splash in puddles and wade through fallen leaves.

In warm weather, lay your baby under a tree and let her enjoy the ultimate mobile. She will be fascinated by the leaves and branches swaying against the backdrop of the sky. Move out into the garden in the summer months and relish in the many new opportunities for play. Fill a child-size pool with bath toys, a toy watering can, and pouring cups and let your baby play away (under close supervision, of course). On sunny days, make rainbows in the garden for your baby. If you have a hose with a fine spray, direct the water high in the air and watch for the rainbow to appear.

Turn going out into an exciting adventure for your baby by taking her on special outings to show her the world outside her window. Travel on a bus or a train and talk to her about all the new sights and sounds. Stores, zoos, and duck ponds also open up intriguing new worlds and encourage her curiosity. A trip to the local park can be equally exciting. Your baby may be too young to run around the park, but by the time she's about six months old, she will enjoy sitting on your lap on a swing and watching the older children play.

MAKING A MESS

Babies love to make a mess, but mess for your baby often equals stress for you. If you really can't stand the mess, then take steps to limit the damage by protecting your baby's clothes with bibs and overalls, putting paper on the floor, and arranging to have messy playtime just before her bath.

Rhymes and rhythm

Whether it's listening to the patterns of your speech as you recite favorite nursery rhymes, or hearing the different rhythms of music, your baby will be stimulated by the different cadences which in turn will develop her language and memory skills.

Nursery rhymes

Introduce your baby to the world of action nursery rhymes. Sing, "Pat-a-cake, pat-a-cake, baker's man," clapping as you sing and using your baby's name when it comes to "put it in the oven for...." Once your baby can sit up, hold her hands and gently rock her to and fro while you sing, "Row, row, row the boat." Your baby will also adore bouncing on your knee to the accompaniment of "Humpty Dumpty." Hold her firmly and pull your knees apart when Humpty Dumpty "has a big fall," letting her drop through your open knees slightly (while still holding on tight!).

Your baby is slowly discovering her body. Help her on this journey of discovery by playing games with her fingers and toes and other parts of her body. Play "Round and round the garden like a teddy bear." Run your finger in a circle around your baby's tummy and give her a tickle under her arm at the end. Once she is familiar with the rhyme, just the anticipation of the tickle at the end will be enough to make her giggle. Use your baby's toes to play "This little piggy." When you get to the last little piggy, say "wee" while you run your fingers up her body and gently tickle her around the neck. Lay your baby down and sing "Itsy Bitsy Spider" while you walk your fingers from her toes up to her head, following the rhythm of the song.

Making music

Bring music into your baby's life by turning on the radio or
putting on a CD and dancing around with her in your arms. You
will be surprised at how quickly she recognizes a familiar tune.
Keep music soothing and entertaining. Your baby will probably
enjoy classical music and gentle pop songs, but may become
upset if you try her out with a heavy rock and roll number. Buy a
CD of children's nursery rhymes and songs for your baby. This is
especially good for keeping your baby happy on long car journeys,
and it will give you some time off as the main entertainer.

SAFE PLAY

Your baby's curiosity is endless, and once she starts to move,
she will be into everything. Rather than constantly saying, "No,"
remove hazards from her path. Check your baby's toys for
safety. Choose sturdy toys that are free of small pieces, which
could break off and injure her or be choked on, and avoid
strings or ribbons longer than 6 in (15 cm), which your baby
could put around her neck.

While you can't ensure that everything he touches is
squeaky clean, try your best to keep toys hygienic. Washable
toys are a bonus and check to make sure that
painted toys are nontoxic.

Your changing baby

Your baby's development

Cherish your baby's journey from helpless infant to independent toddler. Being at his side and helping him grow and develop gives him the stability and love he needs—and is a fascinating experience for you.

Milestones

Don't panic if your baby doesn't lift his head, sit up, or walk as early as other babies. As long as he learns these skills within a reasonable time, there is unlikely to be anything wrong with his development.

Each baby develops at his or her own unique rate so use developmental milestones as guidelines, rather than rules. If he senses that you are anxious for him to achieve more, this may hinder rather than help his development. Rather than angst about what he is or isn't doing, it's more important to understand how your baby develops and encourage him as he experiments with new skills. Do make allowances for your baby if he was born prematurely. If he was several weeks early, he will probably meet early milestones at a later stage than will full-term babies. By around two years, however, he will most likely have caught up.

How your baby learns

The change from helpless newborn to multiskilled one-year-old is truly astounding and your baby's own development is unique, so where another baby may be able to pick up a toy or sit unaided earlier, your baby may learn to make different sounds or understand language before others. By around two years, most differences in learning have usually evened out.

Learning new skills is hard work for your baby, so don't expect him to learn everything at once. For example, while he is putting all his concentration into crawling, he may show little interest in practicing new noises. Similarly, your baby may seem to forget a previously learned skill while he's perfecting a new one. Don't panic—it will all come together in the end.

Avoiding criticism

Rather than fret about what your baby can't do yet, marvel at what he has achieved. It may be frustrating to watch your baby's repeated attempts to master a new skill and his frequent mistakes, but try your best not to criticize him. Trial and error is the key to his development and he learns by constant practice. When your baby masters a new skill, reward him with love and attention rather than candy or gifts. Praising him when he learns to do something new will encourage him and give him the confidence he needs to continue mastering new skills. Bear in mind that your baby will have "off" days. Some days he may seem bright and alert, while on other days he is easily distressed; try to be aware of and responsive to his needs.

From newborn to three months

From the time he is just one month old, your baby's senses are alert. Watch his eyes and head move toward a bright light, and observe how intensely he watches you when he is feeding. He is also gradually getting used to new sights and sounds, but sudden loud noises may make him jump and jerk his limbs out, so try to keep his environment soothing and calm so as not to alarm him.

Responding to your baby

Your baby's first cries are reflex reactions to hunger, discomfort, and pain, but he will soon learn that crying elicits a response from you, and his cries will become more intentional. Pick him up and cuddle him to show him that he is loved and cared for, which will in turn increase his confidence.

Self-discovery

At about three months, your baby is learning rapidly about himself and is particularly fascinated by his hands. Help him on this journey of discovery by holding his hands in front of his face and pointing out his fingers and thumbs, tickling his palms, and gently moving his fingers. Don't try to stop your baby from chewing his hands and fingers, as this is a natural stage in his development. If he uses a pacifier, try to limit the time it's in his mouth so that he can get on with exploring his hands.

BOYS AND GIRLS

Some experts believe that there are noticeable gender differences at even a very early age. It's a common belief that baby boys tend to cry more and need more emotional security, so if your baby boy seems to demand a lot of comforting, don't worry—he may just need extra hugs.

Your baby's developing senses

Your baby's senses are the tools he uses to develop his understanding of the world about him. There are many ways in which you can help him on this journey of discovery and so increase his confidence and wellbeing.

Sight

At one month, your baby's sight is still developing and he can only focus on objects held no more than 6 to 10 in (15 to 25 cm) from his face. In these first few weeks, his attention is drawn to moving objects so hold a toy close to his face, move it slowly in an arc, and watch him follow the object with his eyes. As your baby will spend a lot of time simply lying on his back, putting him under a baby gym will help to keep him visually stimulated. Or attach a plastic mirror to the side of your baby's crib: he will be endlessly fascinated by his own changing expressions, and will be developing his observation skills.

In the first few weeks, your baby's visual development will be stimulated by simple patterns and bold designs in black and white, but from the time he is about three months old, he will show an intense interest in bright objects, so hang a colorful mobile above his crib. You can help him to start recognizing colors by playing with different-colored plastic beakers or building blocks together.

Some experts believe that the more babies are encouraged to look at objects around them, the higher their intelligence will be at four years of age. Walk from room to room and talk to your baby about the things he can see, then stand by the window and point out the trees, cars, and people. Your baby's ability to focus and to use both eyes together is increased by watching moving images, so show him trees blowing in the wind or the laundry flapping on the line.

At about six months, your baby's vision has developed considerably. Feed his ever-increasing curiosity by giving him a selection of bright-colored toys, flash cards, and board books.

Recognizing sounds

At about three months, your baby is more attuned to the sounds around him. Encourage him to identify noises by pointing out different sounds, from the whir of the washing machine to the singing of a bird outside. Point to objects, such as the telephone or the radio, when they make a noise so that your baby expands his understanding of the sounds around him. Increase your baby's ability to locate sound by calling to him from across the room and then seeing if his gaze turns to you. Once your baby starts to identify sounds, he will become excited when he hears comforting ones, such as the bathwater running or a familiar voice.

Smell

From the moment he is born, your baby identifies you by your smell, and if he is breast-fed he will be able to distinguish the smell of your milk from any other mother's. Being aware of this will help you to bond with your baby and develop a unique closeness with him. Your baby's well-developed sense of smell also helps him to learn about his world. He turns his head away from unpleasant smells, and he associates others with comfort. Help him discover new and exciting scents by holding a flower or herb for him to smell.

Taste

Most babies have a sweet tooth. Help your baby develop a more varied palate by introducing him to a wide variety of foods and flavors early on.

Touch

Your baby's sense of touch is incredibly important in his discovery of the world and your older baby enjoys exploring varying textures and shapes. Give him different-textured toys to hold, and talk to him about which one is smooth, soft, furry, or hard. Try to change the toys he plays with from day to day, so that he is constantly stimulated.

Touch also has an important role to play in bonding. Whether through the skin-to-skin contact of breast-feeding or by cradling him close to you, touching helps you and your baby feel at ease with each other. Your physical contact and touch also give your baby a deep sense of security. Stroking him, holding him, and cuddling him will all give him a sense of belonging.

Holding and handling

From his initial unco-ordinated fumbles to the competent manipulation of his toys, your baby is constantly striving to learn how to pick up, hold, and handle his toys and other objects around him. As his ability in this area increases, the world of play opportunities broadens.

The first few months

By three months, your baby may have gained sufficient hand control to hold onto an object. Place a toy in his hand so that he gets used to the sensation of holding, and can develop his gripping skills. At about three to four months, he may start to pick up toys that are close by. Put an easily grasped toy next to him and express your delight when he manages to reach out and pick it up.

Your older baby

Your baby learns to pick up a toy he can see before he learns to look for one that has dropped out of his sight. If he throws all of his toys behind him, put them back in front of him so that he doesn't suddenly find himself without playmates. At about five to six months, he may be able to hold an object in each hand. Give him a small toy to hold in one hand, then put one in his other hand so that he can practice this new skill.

By nine months, your baby may reach out for a toy that is held in front of him. Encourage him to develop his movement by sitting in front of him and holding objects within his reach. Your baby's pincer grasp starts to develop around his ninth month, and he may be able to pick up an object between his finger and thumb. Place a small object in front of him so he can practice perfecting this exciting new skill. Also around nine months, your baby may hold onto his bottle when you feed him. You should still supervise his feeding, however, and don't be tempted to leave him to feed himself.

Hand-eye co-ordination

By around nine months your baby's improved hand-eye co-ordination and greater attention span enable him to play in an increasingly sophisticated way. Help him to develop his hand-eye co-ordination and manual dexterity by rolling a ball to him and encouraging him to push it back to you. Finger foods are also wonderful tools for improving your older baby's hand-eye co-ordination.

Mobility

Your baby learns from top to bottom, so he will hold up his head before he can coordinate his hands and arms, and his legs will be the last part of his body that he learns to control. In no time at all, your newborn baby will start to kick his arms and legs around. This is the beginning of his journey of self-discovery, which will eventually lead to him crawling and walking. Help him on this journey by being aware of how and when your baby learns to manipulate different parts of his body and what you can do to help.

From newborn to crawler

Help your small baby strengthen the muscles in his legs by holding him upright on your lap and letting him step up and down on you and then gently bob him up and down on your knees to help him develop his balancing skills. At about four months, you can start to put him down on his tummy. In this position he may start to lift his arms and legs off the floor, which is his first step in learning how to crawl. Being on his tummy also makes it easier for him to lift his head up, look around, and grasp toys within his reach. Once he is able to control his head, you can also try propping him up on some cushions so that he has an exciting new perspective on the world. Let your baby spend some time each day without clothes so that he can kick and move his limbs about and develop his muscle co-ordination.

Before your baby gains enough control over his lower body to crawl, he may learn how to roll, an exciting step for your baby as it enables him to reach for and grab objects that, before, he could just look at. At around six months your baby will master the art of sitting up. As toppling over is one of the hazards of learning to sit up, some well-placed cushions will give him support. Help your baby's balance by placing a toy a short distance away so that he can practice reaching out for it.

Some time after your baby learns to sit upright, around his ninth month, he may make his first attempt at crawling. Sit a short distance from him and encourage him to come toward you and give him a big cuddle as a reward when he finally manages to reach you. Another added incentive is to place a toy a short distance from him or to give him a pull-along toy with wheels. Once he can crawl around, help him develop an awareness of his body space by encouraging him to crawl over cushions or under the table, to help him appreciate the size of his body in relation to the objects around him.

From standing to walking

As his first birthday approaches, your baby may start to pull himself up with the support of chairs, low tables, and you. Hold onto any furniture he uses to do this so that he has a stable support. You can also help him by placing chairs around the room at regular intervals. Make sure there are no hard edges or unstable surfaces around that could hurt him and discourage him from trying again. A baby walker that he can push around is another great way to help him find his feet. He will be delighted with himself and gain confidence as he moves around the room.

Although your baby may have learned how to stand, he may not yet have mastered the art of sitting back down, but simply fall onto his bottom with a thud. Don't be too alarmed—his bottom is well padded by his diaper and you'll be amazed at how resilient he can be when he tumbles in his excitement.

Once he can pull himself up, he will be eager to start climbing—up steps, onto the bed, or up onto the couch. Don't discourage him, but always supervise him and stand behind him so that you can catch him if he slips. By his first birthday, your baby's world will have opened up dramatically as he becomes more and more mobile. Help him to expand his horizons by giving him plenty of opportunities to practice his new-found walking skills.

When your baby stands up and lets go of his support with one hand, you'll know that his first wobbly step is not far away. However, try not to be impatient for your baby to walk. People love to predict that your standing baby will be walking by the end of next week. The reality can be quite different, and it may be weeks or months before he takes his first step.

Language, speech, and understanding

Your baby is familiar with the sound of your voice before he has even been born and after his birth, it's a source of comfort and learning. Although he is helpless, he absorbs information all the time, so talking to him constantly, explaining what you are doing, and singing him songs will all feed his growing interest and help him on the road to understanding and, eventually, speech.

Early conversations

It's no coincidence that parents tend to revert instinctively to a high-pitched, singsong patter when they talk to their babies, as evidence shows that babies respond to this type of talk extremely positively. So don't feel foolish! At about three months, your baby may start to reward you by cooing back when you talk to him. Those first coos and gurgles require a lot of effort from your baby as they are the result of his gaining control over his tongue movements while he takes in air, which he has learned through weeks of moving his mouth around. Respond to his chatter to make him feel that he is interacting with you and reward his efforts accordingly with big smiles and lots of attention.

Listening and learning

Your baby listens with greater intensity to people talking than to other noises. Chat to him as often as possible to help him identify the patterns of speech that form the basis of language. You will help his grasp of language further by making eye contact when you talk to him and by keeping your speech simple.

Understanding and speech

Your baby's comprehension becomes more sophisticated throughout his first year. Naming objects and people helps him develop his understanding, and by his first birthday he will probably recognize key words and phrases. Until he can talk, he learns to communicate by other means—facial expressions, pointing, and other gestures. Encourage him in these first attempts at communication by responding with smiles, raised eyebrows, and wide eyes.

Help your baby develop his understanding of language by telling him what you are going to do before you do it. For example, explain to him that you are going to run his bath, and then let him watch the water filling up in the bathtub. Consistency from you will help your baby's understanding of vocabulary, so use the same words for the same object all the time to avoid confusion.

At about five to six months, your baby may start to make sounds such as "da" and "ma." Respond with similar noises and have a "baby talk" conversation together. Toward his first birthday, your baby may say his first word. This is likely to be something simple, such as "Mama" or "Dada." Your joint efforts at communicating have paid off! Your one-year-old's capacity for understanding and observing has improved dramatically over the year.

Communication

At about six months, your baby may start to express his emotions and he will watch for your response. He will laugh and smile in delight when he is pleased and show frustration when he is bored. Being aware of his emotions and responding to his needs will give him a sense of self-worth. At about nine months, your baby may learn to signal to you when he wants something. He may hold his arms up when he wants to be picked up, and point to objects that he is interested in. Respond to his signals so that he is encouraged to communicate with you.

MEMORY

Help your baby develop his memory skills by playing the same games with the same toys, using the same words and phrases, and looking at the same picture books again and again.

The world of books and words

It's never too early to introduce your baby to books. Show him flash cards and simple picture books to ignite his interest and increase his familiarity with new words. Point to each picture and tell him what you can see. Eventually your baby will be able to point to the object himself when you name it. Refresh your memory of childhood nursery rhymes. Your baby loves to listen to rhymes, and the repetition of the verses helps his listening skills and develops his memory.

Social development

Your baby craves your love and attention. Responding to him positively, whether as a helpless newborn or an inquisitive baby, gives him the security he needs to develop into a happy, social baby. However, throughout his first year, your baby will show little interest in others outside his close family unit. Even other babies will hold little fascination for him, and he will play alongside, but not with, them. This is quite normal and does not hamper his social development.

Early days

Your baby's first facial grimaces are more likely to be the result of gas than they are a real smile, but at around six weeks he may make his first proper smile. If he gets a positive response, he will reward you with many more smiles. He will become more and more responsive during the first few months of his life and if he is able to illicit a response from you as he coos and chuckles, he will be greatly encouraged in his social development. At about three months, he will show obvious pleasure when you pay him attention, and he is likely to squeal with delight if you tickle him gently. Your baby is increasingly social now, and he delights in company and attention. Enjoy this new stage in his development and watch his interest in the world about him grow.

Your older baby

Your older baby learns that, by mimicking you, he can make you laugh and respond. He will mimic the people closest to him, so if you smile at him when he makes a face, he will learn that moving his mouth into a smile will earn a smile back from you, which in turn helps him feel that he has real control over his social environment. Help his social development by sitting him on your lap and making funny faces, rolling your eyes, and sticking out your tongue. Then watch him try to copy you.

At about six months, your baby has a greater awareness of the world, and he wants to stay close to the most important people in it. You may despair at this time when your previously outgoing baby starts to scream whenever you leave his side. Although it's just a passing phase, this is an important stage in your baby's development (see "Separation anxiety" on page 140). Follow your baby's lead and don't try and force him to socialize with strangers. He will learn soon enough that it is safe to leave your side and venture further afield.

His first birthday

As each month passes, your baby has become more social and responsive and, by his first birthday, he is aware of himself as a separate person. Encourage his growing independence, but be there when he needs a cuddle.

Out and about

Turn a supermarket trip into a learning experience by pointing out all the brightly colored fruits and vegetables and talk to your baby about what you are buying. Ask your older baby to help you choose items at the supermarket. Even if he can't join in the discussion, he will take more of an interest in what is going on, and he will learn about the art of conversation.

Feed your baby's increasing curiosity about the world. Take him out to the park and gather a collection of leaves, twigs, and dandelions. Let him touch and hold each one.

Family matters

Looking after yourself

There's no denying that being a new mother is stressful. Try to accept this and find a way to relieve the stress, whether it's by putting your feet up and watching a video in the evening or doing some therapeutic gardening. Don't feel guilty about having time to yourself. It's important for you and your baby that you feel refreshed rather than frustrated and hemmed in. It's equally important to get plenty of rest to be able to meet the constant demands of a newborn.

Time alone

Occasional breaks from your baby will revive your spirits and help your baby's confidence to grow as he learns that you always return. Try to find some time for yourself each day—even if it's just for a soak in the bath for half an hour while your partner looks after the baby. If you make time for yourself, your baby will come to recognize that this is an important part of family life and you will feel more positive about looking after your baby.

Sometimes it can seem almost impossible to make time for the small, but important, necessities, such as managing to have a shower or sitting down for a cup of tea, but with some strategic planning these can be done. Even if it takes letting your baby cry in his crib for five minutes while you put on your makeup, this won't do him any harm. For a longer break, arrange with your partner for you to have a couple of hours alone during the weekend while he takes the baby out. He will have time to get to know his baby, and you will have some precious time off. Once your baby has a good nighttime routine, you can reclaim some of your lost independence by taking an evening class once a week.

Rest and relaxation

Let the housework take a back seat for the first few weeks after your baby is born. It will be impossible to keep everything in order, and the most important thing now is for you to take it easy and spend time getting to know your baby. Get some much-needed rest by catnapping during the day while your baby is asleep. Or if you find it hard to sleep during the day, just put your feet up and relax when your baby sleeps.

If you get 10 minutes to yourself you can unwind by going to a quiet room, making yourself comfortable, and then using your fingertips to make small, firm, circular movements over your scalp. After a trying day, enjoy a warm evening bath to help you relax, unwind, and get to sleep. Add a few drops of essential oil of lavender to the bath for a wonderfully calming effect and then indulge in a glass of wine, which will help you to unwind—the occasional glass of which won't harm your baby while you're breast-feeding.

Hair and skin care

You may find that your hair falls out more and loses its condition after the birth of your baby. This is the result of your hormones returning to their pre-pregnancy levels. Although it may be distressing, it is just a passing phase. Give yourself a boost by getting your hair cut into a manageable, low-maintenance style.

Take advantage of your baby's toiletries, as these aren't just kind to your baby's skin: they're great for you, too. Baby lotion, shampoo, and bubble bath will all moisturize your skin and hair and leave you feeling silky and smooth.

EATING WELL

Dealing with the 24-hour needs of your new baby can be exhausting, so it's vital that you look after yourself. Keep your energy levels up by eating a balanced diet, enjoying nutritious snacks, and drinking plenty of fluids.

Keeping fit and trim

Don't be in a rush to return to your pre-pregnancy figure. Now is not the time for crash diets, especially if you're breast-feeding. You will eventually lose the extra folds, and the healthiest way to do this is gradually. So be kind to yourself: avoid looking in full-length mirrors for the first few weeks after the birth, and don't depress yourself by trying to squeeze into tight jeans.

Gentle toning exercises will help you get rid of your extra flab and increase your energy levels and, unless you had a cesarean delivery or complicated labor, you can start simple exercises just a few days after the birth. Once you feel able, you may want to keep your mind and body alert by signing up for a postnatal exercise class. Many gyms offer supervised child care, giving you the chance to take time out, get fit, and make new friends. Or if you're really keen, buy an all-terrain stroller that you can comfortably push, and set off for a run. You'll feel better, and your baby will enjoy the change of scene.

You and your partner

A new baby on the scene can often leave someone feeling left out—either Mom or Dad. It's important that you and your partner don't lavish all your attention on your baby and forget to give any to each other. Furthermore, it's easy to let your relationship with your partner slip when you're both so tired that it's an effort just to hold a conversation. However, it's important to make time for each other, so try to get out on a regular basis and spend time just being a couple.

Time together

Spontaneity often goes out the window when a new baby arrives, and you may find that time alone with your partner requires planning. Rather than feeling resentful, try to adapt and plan ahead, so that your time together doesn't become a rare commodity. On a day-to-day basis, letting your baby stay up each night will seriously erode the time that you spend with your partner so ensure that you and your partner have quality time alone by getting your baby into a going-to-bed routine at a reasonable hour.

If you and your partner find that your busy lives leave little time for each other, re-evaluate your schedules and cut back on nonessential commitments. When you do have time alone together, find topics of conversation other than your baby to talk about and make an effort not to abandon all your old rituals, such as playing music or doing the crossword puzzle together.

If sex is the last thing on your mind after childbirth, don't fret or feel guilty. Instead, build up your sex drive gradually by spending time with your partner, just caressing, massaging, and cuddling each other. Sometimes, just enjoying a cuddle on the couch together once your baby is tucked up is enough to help you and your partner remember what it feels like to be a couple.

Time out for your partner

It's important that your partner has time alone, too, so encourage him to go out and see friends on a regular basis and to continue with any not-too-time-consuming hobbies.

Giving him confidence

Your partner may feel left on the sidelines when all of your attention is focused on your baby. Help him to feel involved and close to his baby by asking him to bottle-feed him. If you are breast-feeding, try expressing milk so that he can give him supplementary bottles. Don't criticize your partner's efforts at baby care. Like you, he is on a steep learning curve, and encouraging and helping him will be far more constructive. It's a good idea to give your partner time alone with the baby so that he feels included and can forge his own relationship with his baby.

On the other hand, you may find to your surprise that you're jealous of your partner's blossoming relationship with your baby. This isn't unusual, but rather than sulk, explain to your partner how you feel, and be grateful that he is willing to take an active role in parenting.

Working together

You may feel like you're in a competition with your partner as to who is the most tired. Avoid this additional stress by discussing a division of labor together. For example, if your baby is an early waker, you could take turns getting up with him. Talk to your partner about the roles each of you play and how to deal with issues such as discipline. If you are both on the same wavelength, your baby will feel more secure and you will avoid unnecessary conflict.

Making new friends

**Giving up work and having no one but your baby to talk to
each day can be lonely and isolating so it's important that you
try to build up a local network of other new moms to meet up
with. Before long you will realize that life with your new baby
actually opens up a whole new social world as you find
yourself chatting to people who stop to admire him, or talking
to other new mothers at the pediatrician's office, in the
playground, or at playgroups.**

Where to go

Find out about local mother-and-baby groups so that you and
your baby can get out and socialize with other mothers and
babies. You can share experiences and tips, and you will
probably feel greatly relieved to talk to someone who understands
exactly what you are going through. The local playground is an
ideal place to get to know other mothers. Even if your baby is too
young to be active, he will enjoy watching the other children play.
Go to local parent-and-baby get-togethers. These outings not only
give you the opportunity to meet new people, but they're also a
good way for your baby to make new friends and learn how to
socialize. Seek out local baby classes, such as baby yoga or
music groups. They will be stimulating for your baby, and you
will be stimulated by meeting and chatting with other moms.

Once you start to meet new mothers, you could take the
initiative and arrange a weekly coffee-morning rotation. This is a
particularly good idea in the winter months, when you can't get
out much with your baby. Or invite a few mothers and their
babies over for an informal lunch. If the thought of cooking lunch

for a bevy of moms is just too challenging, then keep it simple rather than stress yourself preparing food. You could ask other mothers to contribute something to the lunch, or just buy prepared food at the grocery store.

Avoid competition

Being a new mom can sometimes feel like being in a competition. Remember that everyone does things in their own way and each baby develops at his own pace, so try to resist comparing your own or your baby's progress to that of others.

Being a single parent

Being a single parent is a difficult and demanding role so it's doubly important to build up a good support network. Forgo your pride and accept help when it is offered. Get to know other single mothers and arrange baby swaps, so that you can enjoy regular time to yourself. Your extended family plays an important role when you're bringing up your baby alone so try to enlist the help of aunts, uncles, and grandparents so that you have some rest and your baby will benefit from forming other close relationships.

Getting help

Accept offers of help gratefully. Don't be embarrassed to say yes to help, or feel like this is an admission of failure. You need and deserve time off, so hand over the reins and enjoy yourself.

Lightening the load

If you're lucky enough to have extended family living close by, don't turn down offers of help, and don't feel reluctant to ask for assistance. You need some time to yourself, and your baby will have the chance to forge close bonds with other family members. If willing family members aren't nearby, get some help—even for just a couple of hours or afternoons a week—from a babysitter, who can mind your baby while you take care of household chores or just have a nap.

Evenings out

Make evenings out with your partner worry-free by choosing a babysitter who has plenty of experience with small babies. If you can't get a suitable family member or friend to look after your baby, ask other local mothers if they can recommend someone. You could arrange a babysitting rotation with another mother, so that you and your partner can go out while you leave a trustworthy parent with your baby. Or ask around about a babysitting circle in your area, in which groups of parents take turns babysitting. Make sure that your babysitter is familiar with your baby's routines and has everything she or he needs, such as phone numbers, feeding equipment, and diapers.

Life around your baby

When your new baby comes along, it can seem hard to fit other people into your life. Your little bundle can take over and allow little time for you to keep in touch with friends and family. However, it is important for you to take time to step back and spend time with adults—this will help you stay sane and will form a valuable support system.

Friends

Becoming a mother, meeting new people, and developing new interests doesn't mean you have to abandon your old friends, but you may need to make more of an effort to stay in touch. If you're just too tired during the early weeks and months to get out and see people, make the effort to give friends a call so that you don't lose valuable contact. If you arrange to see friends away from home, especially if you are at home all day with your baby, you can spend time in another environment and stay in touch with old friends.

Grandparents

Next to you and your partner, your baby's grandparents are likely to be his most important source of affection and security and, as they are unlikely to be under the same pressures as you, they can offer your baby a different and special view of the world. Your baby's relationship with his grandparents can be an important bond in his life so let your parents spend time with your baby, and if they offer to look after him, accept the invitation gratefully.

Of course, there is always room for conflict, for instance, if your parents think they know best when it comes to your baby. Avoid confrontation or a falling out by being clear about the ground rules when they are looking after him. Don't feel you have to pay heed to all their advice, but try not to offend—a simple, "I'll remember that" is all that is required. Conversely, your parents may be wary of interfering too much in your new life, so let them know that you want them to be involved by getting them to spend time with your baby and inviting them on special days out. Your parents' experience, love for their grandchild, and spare time can be invaluable to you and your baby.

Siblings

Sibling rivalry is a common problem when a new baby arrives. Take steps to avoid this by giving your older child as much attention as possible so that she doesn't feel that her place in the family has been usurped by the new arrival. Don't feel bewildered if your other child doesn't show immediate love for his new brother or sister. Just like you, she needs some time to get used to the idea of a new family member, and don't forget that the baby's arrival will have been more of a shock for her than for you.

Involving your older child

Help your older child to feel part of the new family set-up by letting her help at bath time or other baby-related times. For example, you could give her small tasks to make her feel involved and helpful, such as passing you the cotton balls when you are changing the baby's diaper. Be careful not to make your older child feel that she has to help with the baby, but don't turn down her help if she offers. Don't ever leave your older child in charge of your baby. This is unsafe, and it's unfair to her and to the baby.

Avoiding jealousy

Avoid jealous feelings from siblings by encouraging your older children to get to know their new brother or sister. They will probably be over the moon once the baby starts to respond and smile at them. Heaps of attention paid to the baby may make an older child feel jealous, but don't go to the other extreme of almost ignoring your baby, or her sibling may well be confused about how she should respond to the new arrival. Help your older child feel relaxed with her new brother or sister by encouraging her to talk, play with, and hold (under your supervision) the baby.

As your new baby will no doubt receive presents from friends and family, make sure her siblings don't feel left out by giving them each a present from their new brother or sister.

Dividing your time

A new baby in the family can make it difficult to give your other children as much time as you would like. Try not to hold your baby all the time. When he is asleep, put him down and spend some one-to-one time with each child.

Returning to work

You may have planned to stay at home with your baby indefinitely, but find after a few months that you're dissatisfied with being a full-time mom, in which case you could consider a more rewarding division of your time. Being happy and fulfilled will be best for all of you, so don't beat yourself up with guilt about your needs and desires. On the other hand, if you have returned to work, but find that stress, guilt, and tiredness are wearing you down, don't feel that you've failed if you have to change your plans.

Child care

Carefully consider child-care options before returning to work. Some parents choose a day-care center because they feel their baby benefits from the company of other babies, while others prefer to keep their child at home under the one-to-one care of a nanny. Whatever your feelings, research child-care facilities thoroughly before making a choice. Find out about staff-to-child ratios at day-care centers, get references from other parents, and don't be afraid to ask plenty of questions before signing up. If you are considering taking on an individual to look after your baby in her home, ask her how many other children she has in her care and whether she picks up extra children after school. Find out about the daily routine that is followed at any facility or by a nanny.

Getting a relative to look after your baby when you return to work may seem like an attractive and cheap option, but be aware of potential pitfalls. It can be tricky to be businesslike with a relative, and he or she may take it personally if you tell them what to do.

Before you return to work, arrange for you and your baby to spend some time together with his caregiver before you leave him alone with her. Once you start work, make sure that you pick your baby up promptly from his caregiver and don't rush him off to bed as soon as possible—even if you're tired, try to spend some quality time with him at the end of each day.

Index